THE EVERYTHING®
JUMBO
BOOK OF
LARGE-PRINT
WORD SEARCHES
VOLUME 2

160 supersized puzzles for hours of entertainment

Charles Timmerman
Founder of Funster.com

Adams Media
New York London Toronto Sydney New Delhi

Adams Media
An Imprint of Simon & Schuster, Inc.
100 Technology Center Drive
Stoughton, Massachusetts 02072

An Everything® Series Book.

Everything® and everything.com® are registered trademarks of Simon & Schuster, Inc.

First Adams Media trade paperback edition September 2022

ADAMS MEDIA and colophon are trademarks of Simon & Schuster.

For information about special discounts for bulk purchases, please contact Simon & Schuster Special Sales at 1-866-506-1949 or business@simonandschuster.com.

The Simon & Schuster Speakers Bureau can bring authors to your live event. For more information or to book an event contact the Simon & Schuster Speakers Bureau at 1-866-248-3049 or visit our website at www.simonspeakers.com.

Manufactured in the United States of America

10 9 8 7 6 5 4 3 2 1

ISBN 978-1-5072-1978-2

Many of the designations used by manufacturers and sellers to distinguish their products are claimed as trademarks. Where those designations appear in this book and Simon & Schuster, Inc., was aware of a trademark claim, the designations have been printed with initial capital letters.

Contains material adapted from the following titles published by Adams Media, an Imprint of Simon & Schuster, Inc.: *The Everything® Large-Print Word Search Book* by Jennifer Edmondson, copyright © 2010, ISBN 978-1-4405-0319-1; *The Everything® Large-Print Word Search Book, Volume 2* by Charles Timmerman, copyright © 2011, ISBN 978-1-4405-1025-0; and *The Everything® Large-Print Word Search Book, Volume 3* by Charles Timmerman, copyright © 2011, ISBN 978-1-4405-2737-1.

Contents

Puzzles

A CHORUS LINE

AVENUE Q

BILLY ELLIOT

CATS

CHICAGO

EVITA

GREASE

GUYS AND DOLLS

HAIRSPRAY

LES MISÉRABLES

LION KING

LITTLE MERMAID

MAMMA MIA!

MARY POPPINS

MISS SAIGON

MY FAIR LADY

OLIVER

OUR HOUSE

PHANTOM

PRODUCERS

RENT

ROCK OF AGES

SOUTH PACIFIC

WEST SIDE STORY

WICKED

Broadway Musicals

```
E O G A C I H C A T S S T N
M G R E A S E S U O H R U O
A Y E D G P L I O N K I N G
M S N I P P O P Y R A M Y I
M E T Q S R E C U D O R P A
A L G U Y S A N D D O L L S
M B C O Z P H A N T O M M S
I A Y L Y A R P S R I A H S
A R B I L L Y E L L I O T I
V E P V J I D E K C I W E M
E S X E N I L S U R O H C A
N I J R S E G A F O K C O R
U M D T M Y F A I R L A D Y
E S S O U T H P A C I F I C
Q E V I T A Q E L C I L G E
W L I T T L E M E R M A I D
```

Solution on Page 328

ACCOUNTS	FEES
ATMS	FINANCIAL
BALANCE	INTEREST
BILLS	INVESTMENT
BONDS	LENDING
BRANCH	LINES
BUSINESS	MANAGER
CAPITAL	MONEY
CASH	MORTGAGE
CHANGE	NATIONAL
CHECKING	OVERDRAWN
COINS	PAYMENT
CREDIT	RATE
CURRENCY	ROBBERY
CUSTOMERS	SECURITY
DEBT	TELLER
DEPOSITS	VAULT
DRAFT	WITHDRAWAL
ECONOMY	

```
F E E S R E L L E T H E H D
M O R T G A G E H R C Y S R
N Z G N I K C E H C N C W A
A Y T U W L A I C N A N I F
T M L O I A I N T E R E S T
I O U C L W R C L O B R E N
O N A C I A C D A S O R C E
N O V A N R U E R S Y U U M
A C S E E D S G C E H C R Y
L E N D S H T T N N V K I A
A E I E L T O O I I A O T P
T T O B L I M F K S D L Y L
I A C T I W E E U U O N A U
P R O B B E R Y N B I P E B
A A B O N D S C A T M S E L
C H A N G E R E G A N A M D
```

Solution on Page 328

AISLES

BABY CARE

BANANAS

BEER

BEVERAGES

BOXED

BREAD

BULK

CART

CLERK

COOKIES

COUPONS

DEBIT CARD

DELI

DISPLAYS

EGGS

FLOWERS

FRESH

FROZEN FOODS

GENERIC

LIGHT BULB

MANAGER

MEDICINE

MILK

MUSTARD

PARKING LOT

PEANUT BUTTER

PICKLES

PROMOTIONS

PURCHASE

SEASONAL

SHOPPERS

SHOPPING

SOAP

VEGETABLES

WAX PAPER

Grocery Store

```
B U L K C V G E N E R I C H
R M U B L E R A C Y B A B S
E E I S E G A R E V E B H E
A D T L R E P A P X A W S R
D I O T K T R E G A N A M F
F C L S U A I L E D H B R S
L I G H T B U L B C A O N Y
O N N O M L T Y R N Z O S A
W E I P U E A U A E I C E L
E S K P S S P N N T C G L P
R E R I T D A F O A G O S S
S I A N A S O M R S E K I I
Y K P G R O O T S O A P A D
B O X E D R A C T I B E D F
D O F S P S H O P P E R S D
Z C O U P O N S E L K C I P
```

Solution on Page 328

BAKERY

BAKING

BAKLAVA

BREAD

BUTTER

CAKES

CHEF

CHOCOLATE

COOKING

CREAM PUFF

CROISSANT

CRUST

CUSTARD

DANISH

DESSERT

DISH

DOUGHNUT

EGGS

FILLING

FLAKY

FLOUR

FOOD

FRENCH

ITALIAN

MILK

NAPOLEON

OVEN

PETIT FOUR

PIES

RESTAURANT

SCONE

SHORTENING

STRUDEL

SWEET

TARTS

TORTE

```
P I E S W C O V E N F T H L
H T U N H G U O D L D O O F
Y Y N A P O L E O N C R Y B
B I C A V X C U R O H T B A
U A A H S A R A O H S E R K
T S K F E S L K T D I T E E
T F E I F F I K N T N A A R
E F S L N N N O A R A L D Y
R U W L G G W L R B D O R S
S P E I H S I D U C I C A G
T M E N V A Y K A L F O T G
R A T G N I N E T R O H S E
A E F Z T R E S S E D C U N
T R U O F T I T E P G E C O
C C O K L E D U R T S U R C
H M I L K H C N E R F M S S
```

Solution on Page 328

AMMO

ANGLE

BACKDOOR

BANKROLL

BET

BLUFF

BOMB

BONE

BUY THE POT

CALL

CHECK

CROSSFIRE

DECLARE

DECLOAK

DOWN CARD

DUMP

FLOP

FLUSH

GARBAGE

GIVING AIR

HAMMER

HIJACK

ISOLATION

KICKER

KITTY

LOOSE

LOWBALL

MUCK

MUPPET

OFFSUIT

PASSIVE

POKER FACE

PUSH

RAISE

SANDBAG

SHILL

SHOWDOWN

SPLIT

STAKES

STAND PAT

```
P F L O P M U D E C L A R E
U V R I A G N I V I G O L S
S P L I T I U S F F O B L I
H I J A C K C U M D O L I A
T S N J L L O R K N A B H R
P O K E R F A C E B M B S E
P L P B U N A R W D M H U M
F A E E G B I O N O O G L M
K T S L H F L K B W S L F A
Q I E S S T A P D N A T S H
R O T S I O Y O B C N E T F
E N O T L V W U T A D P A F
K R A C Y N E F B R B P K U
C X E G A B R A G D A U E L
I D T P T G Z E T I G M S B
K C E H C S L O O S E K O Q
```

Solution on Page 329

BELLY FLOP

BIKINI

BREASTSTROKE

CABANA

CAN OPENER

CANNONBALL

DEEP END

DIVING BOARD

DOGGIE PADDLE

DRAIN

FINS

HIGH DIVE

HOT TUB

KIDDIE POOL

LIFEGUARD

LIFESAVER

MARCO POLO

PARTY

RAFT

SHALLOW END

SNORKEL

SPLASH

SUNBLOCK

SUNSCREEN

SWIMSUIT

TAN

TOWEL

TRUNKS

TUBE

WADING POOL

WATER WINGS

WAVE

WET

Fun in the Pool

```
N E E R C S N U S P L A S H
N C L O O P G N I D A W I W
B A W D I D E E P E N D N A
E N A T D R S W I M S U I T
L N B R E A S T S T R O K E
L O C A N O P E N E R S I R
Y N O G D B I E B N N H B W
F B L P R G P U I I K A H I
L A O S E N T A A G H L I N
O L P N V I I R R Q G L G G
P L O O A V D B U T T O H S
W E C R S I M D F E Y W D N
A W R K E D K A I W W E I I
V O A E F T R U N K S N V F
E T M L I F E G U A R D E D
S U N B L O C K A N A B A C
```

Solution on Page 329

ARITHMETIC	GLEE CLUB
ASSEMBLY	HOMEWORK
AUTOMOTIVE	HONOR ROLL
CHALKBOARD	KINDERGARTEN
CHEERLEADERS	MARCHING BAND
COLOR GUARD	PEER TUTORING
COMMENCEMENT	PROBATION
DANCE TEAM	QUIZ
DEAN'S LIST	REPORT CARD
DIPLOMA	SOCIAL STUDIES
DRAMA CLUB	SYMPHONIC BAND
FINAL	TARDY
FRESHMAN	
GEOMETRY	

At School

```
U P A P S B U L C A M A R D
C E S R E D A E L R E E H C
O E S O I M A E T E C N A D
L R E B D R A C T R O P E R
O T M A U F R E S H M A N C
R U B T T D I P L O M A X I
G T L I S B U L C E E L G T
U O Y O L L O R R O N O H E
A R D N A B G N I H C R A M
R I Q U I Z K R O W E M O H
D N A B C I N O H P M Y S T
Y G G E O M E T R Y E U F I
D E A N S L I S T C N Z I R
R K I N D E R G A R T E N A
A K G E V I T O M O T U A K
T J C H A L K B O A R D L Z
```

Solution on Page 329

ANNUAL

ANTHER

BASAL PLATE

CASTINGS

CHLOROPHYLL

CORM

COTYLEDON

CROWN

EMBRYO

ENDOSPERM

FERTILIZATION

FILAMENT

GRAFTING

LOAM

MONOCOT

ORGANIC MATTER

OVARY

OVULE

PETIOLE

PHLOEM CELLS

PHOTOSYNTHESIS

PLANTLETS

POTASSIUM

RECEPTACLE

SAND

SEED

SEPAL

SILT

SPORE

STAMEN

TUBER

VEGETATIVE

VERMICULITE

```
R G R A F T I N G Y D P U N
V E P H L O E M C E L L S L
E E T A L P L A S A B A I S
G G R T N C S T A M E N S E
E A T M A T O E L O I T E P
T L N O I M H T R Q Z L H A
A U U N C C E Y O D E T L
T D G V U O U I R L P T N C
I S N M O A N L N E E S Y R
V Y R A V O L O I A B D S O
E N D O S P E R M T G U O W
M K E L C A T P E C E R T N
B F E R T I L I Z A T I O N
R T S L L Y H P O R O L H C
Y C O R M U I S S A T O P N
O M R F I L A M E N T L I S
```

Solution on Page 329

BRAND

BUSINESS

CALIFORNIA

CAMERAS

CARTRIDGE

COMPETITOR

COMPUTERS

COPIER

DESKTOPS

DIGITAL

FAX

GARAGE

GLOBAL

HARDWARE

INKJET

KEYBOARD

LAPTOPS

MONITORS

NETWORKING

OFFICE

PALO ALTO

PAPER

PRINTERS

SALES

SCANNER

SERVERS

SOFTWARE

STORAGE

SUPPORT

TECHNOLOGY

TONER

```
N X D E S K T O P S T M G T
C O P I E R A W D R A H A R
J M O N I T O R S E S H R O
S J G N I K R O W T E N A P
R I N K J E T T D U R W G P
E E C P O L K I S P V B E U
T P N A A L G T A M E U G S
N E D O L I X E L O R S D T
I R L R T I A P E C S I I O
R A N A A N F M S I D N R R
P W L Y G O L O N H C E T A
A T D N A R B C R R D S R G
O F F I C E O Y I N E S A E
S O N S C A N N E R I P C B
M S A R E M A C D K S A A C
S P O T P A L A B O L G X P
```

Solution on Page 330

ADVERTISING

BIG APPLE

BRONX ZOO

CARNEGIE HALL

CENTRAL PARK

CITICORP

EAST RIVER

GRAND CENTRAL

HOLLAND TUNNEL

HUDSON RIVER

KNICKS

LAGUARDIA

LINCOLN CENTER

MADISON AVENUE

METS

NEVER SLEEPS

PARK AVENUE

SKYSCRAPERS

TAMMANY HALL

TEXTILE

TOURISM

TRAFFIC

YANKEES

```
I T E X T I L E W M O J Z N
C A R N E G I E H A L L D E
U M Z L A G U A R D I A S V
E M H U D S O N R I V E R E
U A B C T O U R I S M E E R
N N I P J K B A S O T B P S
E Y G R A N D C E N T R A L
V H A O D C M A E A R O R E
A A P C S T S C K V A N C E
K L P I H T N M N E F X S P
R L L T R L E J A N F Z Y S
A A E I O X G M Y U I O K K
P L V C K M Y Q D E C O S C
C E N T R A L P A R K C H I
R I A D V E R T I S I N G N
L E N N U T D N A L L O H K
```

Solution on Page 330

ALGERIA	JAPAN
ARGENTINA	KENYA
AUSTRALIA	MACEDONIA
BOLIVIA	NEW ZEALAND
BULGARIA	NORTH KOREA
COSTA RICA	PAKISTAN
DENMARK	PANAMA
ECUADOR	PARAGUAY
FINLAND	RUSSIA
FRANCE	SAUDI ARABIA
GERMANY	SOUTH AFRICA
GREENLAND	SWITZERLAND
HAITI	VENEZUELA
HISTORY	YEMEN
INDIA	ZIMBABWE
JAMAICA	

```
A I V I L O B N E M E Y S E
J Y A L E U Z E N E V A C K
C Z I M B A B W E J U N Z K
G E R M A N Y Z M D A L D R
Y R O D A U C E I R C P N A
A R S O U T H A F R I C A M
U A I S S U R L B A R A L N
G I A C I A M A J U A N R E
A R A T B C N N Y S T I E D
R A E I S F X D T T S T Z H
A G A E R O K H T R O N T I
P L Y I N E K H S A C E I S
M U N N H L G P A L U G W T
N B E D D N A L N I F R S O
P A K I S T A N A A T A C R
P A N A M A C E D O N I A Y
```

Solution on Page 330

ALIENS	GAUNTLET
AMBUSH	JOUST
ARCADE	MAPPY
ASTEROIDS	MARIO BROS.
ATARI	METAL SLUG
BATMAN	PAC-MAN
BATTLEZONE	PINBALL
CENTIPEDE	PLAY
COMMANDO	PONG
CONTRA	QIX
CRAZY TAXI	SIMPSONS
DEFENDER	STAR WARS
DIG DUG	TEKKEN
DUCK HUNT	TETRIS
FROGGER	TRON
GALAXIAN	

```
N E L S O R B O I R A M J A
W T E K K E N G X I Q G P Z
H N A M C A P U A M B U S H
L U E N O Z E L T T A B S D
R H T E T R I S Y C F D R I
E K A S O I J L Z Y I I A X
D C L I I R X A A O P P W L
N U I M I A R T R D I P R I
E D E P I T N E C N G W A D
F J N S N A T M B A A R T M
E P S O M S P A L M U E S E
D O C N A P L A Y M N D U V
Q N N S Y L X W M O T A O D
R G U D G I D B Y C L C J K
A C S G A F R O G G E R I Q
T R O N A M T A B C T A M G
```

Solution on Page 330

BALDERDASH

BATTLESHIP

CANDY LAND

CHECKERS

CHESS

CHUTES AND LADDERS

CLUE

CONNECT FOUR

CRANIUM

GUESS WHO?

LIFE

MEMORY GAME

MONOPOLY

MOUSE TRAP

OPERATION

PAY DAY

PICTIONARY

RISK

RUMMIKUB

SCATTERGORIES

SCRABBLE

SEQUENCE

SORRY

TABOO

TRIVIAL PURSUIT

TWISTER

YAHTZEE

Board Games

```
S R D F S S E H C L U E T T
R U N E E C N E U Q E S H S
E M A G Y R O M E M Y H B N
D M L Q P A H O O B A T A P
D I Y R Y B W N P C H I L K
A K D E R B S O E H T N D P
L U N T A L S P R E Z P E I
D B A S N E E O A C E A R H
N Z C I O B U L T K E R D S
A I R W I R G Y I E F T A E
S C A T T E R G O R I E S L
E J N Z C N Q Y N S L S H T
T R I V I A L P U R S U I T
U A U E P A Y D A Y T O P A
H G M N M O K H M F Y M Z B
C O N N E C T F O U R I S K
```

Solution on Page 331

PUZZLES • 31

AMHERST	JOHNS HOPKINS
APPLICATION	LAW SCHOOL
BACHELOR	LEHIGH
BAYLOR	LIBERAL ARTS
BRANDEIS	NOTRE DAME
CARLETON	PRINCETON
COLLEAGUES	RESEARCHERS
CURRICULUM	SCHOLARSHIPS
DARTMOUTH	SWARTHMORE
DEPARTMENTS	TEACHERS
DOCTORATE	TUFTS
DUKE	USC
EXAM	WELLESLEY
FEDERAL	WILLIAMS
GRINNELL	

College Life

```
T F W R C S I E D N A R B H
S E I J S P G A W D C O A G
R D L O U I D U K E O L P I
E E L H N H E M K P L Y P H
H R I N O S T U B A L A L E
M A A S T R A L A R E B I L
A L M H R A R U C T A S C H
C L S O E L O C H M G L A T
A E R P D O T I E E U O T U
R N E K A H C R L N E O I O
L N H I M C O R O T S H O M
E I C N E S D U R S L C N T
T R A S R E H C R A E S E R
O G E E R O M H T R A W S A
N O T E C N I R P E X A M D
S T F U T Y E L S E L L E W
```

Solution on Page 331

PUZZLES • **33**

ALLOY	ERROR
ASSAY	EURO
BASE METAL	FACE VALUE
BRASS	GOLD
BRONZE	GRADING
BULLION	LUSTER
CAMEO	MEDALLIONS
CARAT	MINT
CENT	MONEY
CIRCULATED	MOTTO
COINS	NICKEL
COLLECTION	OBVERSE
CONDITION	PATINA
COPPER	PAYMENT
CURRENCY	PROOF
DATE	QUARTER
DESIGN	RARE
DIME	SILVER
EAGLE	TOKENS
ENGRAVER	TRADE

```
F R A L A T E M E S A B G S
R E T R A U Q D E S I G N C
E V N O I T I D N O C O U L
V C O P P E R A R O I R E Y
L A I R E T S U L L R K E E
I M L E M F E L L E C E L N
S E L T I A E A N I U S G O
D O U A N C D C N G L R A M
B J B D T E Y E O P A E E O
R R N I M V M L M D T V R T
A S O I T A D Y I E E B R T
S N D N S L C N A T D O O O
S E I N Z U G A I P N A R Z
A K I T R E V A R G N E R B
Y O W Z A L L O Y A X K C T
C T S H E P R O O F T W W I
```

Solution on Page 331

AIR MATTRESS

ANIMALS

BACKYARD

BEACH

BOOTS

CABIN

CAMPFIRE

CAMPSITE

DOME

DUTCH OVEN

FIRST AID KIT

FOIL MEALS

HIKING

KINDLING

KNOT TYING

LANTERN

MESS KIT

MOUNTAINS

NATIONAL PARK

NATURE

OVERNIGHT

POLES

RETREAT

ROPE

SHELTER

SLEEPING BAG

STAKES

SWIMMING

TRAIL MIX

WATER PURIFIER

WINTER

```
C A B I N K C A M P S I T E
K I N D L I N G W L E P O R
H I K I N G L O A J Q O S U
K T F J M N R E T N A L N T
K R I I M A M Q E T E E I A
T A A N R L L R R E Y S A N
G I G P I S I S P K S I T T
N L K O L F T I U E T H N H
I M F S P A N A R M O C U G
M I R M S G N T I O O A O I
M X A E B E T O F D B E M N
I C Z A T A M H I R K B X R
W J G Z M L L R E T N I W E
S C O R N R E T R E A T T V
M M I D U T C H O V E N U O
B A C K Y A R D S T A K E S
```

Solution on Page 331

APRON

BARBECUE SAUCE

BUNS

CHARBROIL

CHARCOAL

CHICKEN

CORN ON THE COB

FIRE

FLAME

FORK

FRUIT

GRILL

HAMBURGER

HOT DOG

KETCHUP

KNIFE

MACARONI SALAD

MAYONNAISE

MEAT

MUSTARD

NAPKIN

PICNIC TABLE

PLATE

POTATO CHIPS

POTATO SALAD

PRONGS

SEASONING

SMOKE

SODA

SPOON

STEAK

TABLECLOTH

WOOD CHIPS

Family Barbecue

```
F C F Z J W O O D C H I P S
P R O N G S P O O N B D I S
F B A R B E C U E S A U C E
M L W W N K G F B L P D N A
M U A L A O C R A H C A I S
P E S M D M N S D H H L C O
P L A T E S O T I E L A T N
A P O T A T O C H I P S A I
E H S O A R K A R E O I B N
R N C T J E D G S D C N L G
I A O S N O R P A T M O E F
F P E H A M B U R G E R B R
O K F H T O L C E L B A T U
R I I L I O R B R A H C K I
K N N E S I A N N O Y A M T
H R K E T C H U P Z A M G E
```

Solution on Page 332

PUZZLES • 39

ALBUM	PAPERBOARD
ATHLETE	PERSON
BASEBALL	PICTURE
BOXING	PLAYERS
BUBBLE GUM	PRISTINE
CARTOONS	RACING
COLLECTOR	RARE
COMIC BOOK	ROOKIE
CONDITION	SCARCITY
EBAY	SELL
FLEER	SETS
FOIL	SPORTS
FOOTBALL	STATISTICS
GAMES	TELEVISION
GOLF	TOPPS
HOBBY	TRADING
HOCKEY	UPPER DECK
IMAGE	VALUABLE
MINT	WRAPPER
PACK	

```
K D R F O I L E I K O O R S
C S C O N D I T I O N R C G
A T A O T E L E V I S I O N
P R T T R C S P P O T L R I
Y O H B A S E L L S F L A X
E P L A D P D L I K D A C O
K S E L I I R T L O G B I B
C C T L N C A M Y O U E N L
O A E E G T O U B B C S G A
H R L D S U B B B C A A W S
P C B A R R R L O I R B R R
E I A Z E E E A H M T M A E
R T U R E G P E D O O I P Y
S Y L B U E A P L C O N P A
O G A M E S P M U F N T E L
N Y V R A R E N I T S I R P
```

Solution on Page 332

BERRY PIE

BONBONS

BRANDY SNAPS

BROWNIES

BUBBLE GUM

CANDY BARS

CHERRY PIE

CONFECTIONERY

COUGH DROP

CREAM PIES

FLAVORINGS

FONDUE

GUMDROPS

GUMMI BEARS

HOREHOUND

JELLY BEAN

MELON

MILKSHAKE

ROCK CANDY

SOUR CANDIES

SPONGE CAKE

STREUSEL

SUGAR CANDY

SUNDAE

TRUFFLES

WHIPPED CREAM

```
Y J F S E I N W O R B B B S N
D R M I L K S H A K E U J B
N B E R R Y P I E Q N B Q J
A G L N R R C P N D R B I E
C U O M O C Q P A A E L P L
R M N S C I D E N S K E O L
A M C E K L T D C E A G R Y
G I R I C E Y C H L C U D B
U B E D A S F R E F E M H E
S E A N N U O E R F G D G A
N A M A D E N A R U N R U N
O R P C Y R D M Y R O O O M
B S I R B T U I P T P P C J
N T E U A S E D I R S S I D
O I S O R H O R E H O U N D
B A I S S G N I R O V A L F
```

BASKETS

BIBLE

CANDY

CHOCOLATE

CHURCH

COLORED EGGS

DYE

EASTER BUNNY

EASTER DRESS

EGG HUNT

FAMILY

FEAST

FESTIVE

FLOWERS

FOOD

GAMES

GIFTS

GOOD FRIDAY

JELLY BEANS

RABBIT

RESURRECTION

RIBBONS

SPRING BREAK

SUNDAY

```
S U T J O B A S K E T S F V
B N B R T D O G G D S E U E
Z C O A Z G Y G R E A Y X J
S H Z B Z V H E R S K A T G
C O F B B U O D T A S D R T
A C O I N I R E E M R I T E
N O I T C E R R U S E R P J
D L W R T B B O L N W F H D
Y A V S U G T L J A O D O L
A T A N N D I O N E L O D G
D E N I G D Z C V B F O O G
N Y R G R Q H I E Y O G T I
U P J Y P U T T Y L I M A F
S J V W R S Y L D L B A W T
Q X E C E B G A M E S I U S
W X H F X C T M C J V Z B N
```

Solution on Page 332

ALBANIA

AUTOBAHN

BOAT

BULGARIA

CASTLE

CROISSANT

CZECH REPUBLIC

ESTONIA

HOTEL

IRON CURTAIN

ITALY

LIECHTENSTEIN

LITHUANIA

MALTA

MONT BLANC

NIGHTLIFE

NORWAY

OKTOBERFEST

PARIS

PASSPORT

SAN MARINO

SCANDINAVIA

SLOVAKIA

SWITZERLAND

UNITED KINGDOM

VATICAN CITY

VISA

WIMBLEDON

YUGOSLAVIA

```
V I S A I K A V O L S T L M
B U L G A R I A I N A B L A
N N D N A L R E Z T I W S L
C I L B U P E R H C E Z C T
P T E Y U G O S L A V I A A
A E F T T P A R I S T R N G
S D I I S M Y L A T I O D T
S K L C E N O Q L L W N I N
P I T N F H E N I E I C N A
O N H A R A S T T F M U A S
R G G C E B T H H B B R V S
T D I I B O O O U C L T I I
A O N T O T N T A M E A A O
O M E A T U I E N V D I N R
B A T V K A A L I E O N L C
Y A W R O N I R A M N A S L
```

Solution on Page 333

ALBATROSS

ANDY NORTH

BACK NINE

BEN HOGAN

BOBBY JONES

COREY PAVIN

DICK MAYER

FRONT NINE

GARY PLAYER

HALE IRWIN

HOLE IN ONE

JACK FLECK

JERRY PATE

KEN VENTURI

LEE JANZEN

LEE TREVINO

LOU GRAHAM

NANCY LOPEZ

NICK PRICE

PATTY BERG

TIGER WOODS

TOM WATSON

Go Golf

```
J E N O S T A W M O T P F A
K C E L F K C A J N O B F L
N D O N I V E R T E E L R B
R H T R O N Y D N A B D O A
K E N V E N T U R I O I N T
Z E P O L Y C N A N B C T R
X J E R R Y P A T E B K N O
N I W R I E L A H U Y M I S
E N I N K C A B V R J A N S
Z B E N H O G A N I O Y E K
N I L H O L E I N O N E A Z
A D G A R Y P L A Y E R O R
J T I G E R W O O D S F F U
E C I R P K C I N R F Y G I
E R Z I P A T T Y B E R G I
L O U G R A H A M G D D O D
```

Solution on Page 333

PUZZLES • **49**

BAGELS

BOLOGNA

BREAD

CAVIAR

CHEESES

CHICKEN

COFFEE

COLD CUTS

COOKIES

COUNTER

DELICIOUS

DIPS

DRINKS

FINE FOODS

GERMAN

GROCERY

HAM

JEWISH

KOSHER

LUNCH

MEATS

MILK

NEW YORK

NUMBER

OLIVES

ORDER

PASTRAMI

PICKLE

SALAMI

SANDWICHES

SAUSAGE

SHOP

STORE

TEA

TUNA

TURKEY

WINE

```
S Y T G L I M A R T S A P O
K O S H E R K S N U M B E R
C O O K I E S P O G C K N D
Q U F R N B Y I S D O W I E
F P T O D I C D A H F L W R
T I U Y K I R E N A F S O J
D C N W L E R D D M E N E B
H K A E T B N S W V E W R P
G L D N F C T Z I K I A V O
R E U X A O K L C S E E T H
O O N V R L O I H T G S N S
C U I E I D H D E A L A N H
E A Z M D C S E S E E H C C
R Y E K R U T U G E R M A N
Y B B U G T A A W F U K E U
I M A L A S B K C B E H M L
```

Solution on Page 333

BENNY GOODMAN

BILLIE HOLIDAY

BOCCHERINI

BRITTEN

BURT BACHARACH

ELGAR

FATS WALLER

HANDEL

HARRY RUBY

HAYDN

IRA GERSHWIN

JOHN LENNON

JOHN STROMBERG

JULE STYNE

LORENZ HART

MILT JACKSON

MOZART

PAGANINI

PAUL MCCARTNEY

ROSSINI

SIBELIUS

STEPHEN FOSTER

STEVIE WONDER

TOMMY DORSEY

```
M L T O M M Y D O R S E Y Z Z
N O Z N I W H S R E G A R I
A R N L M K S W R N D Y A H
M E O E O C T L E I E E G G
D N S D Z Q E A L S N N L R
O Z K N A D P O L I Y T E E
O H C A R A H C A B T R U B
G A A H T E E P W E S A H M
Y R J R I X N A S L E C A O
N T T L O Y F G T I L C R R
N Y L H V S O A A U U M R T
E I I Q G V S N F S J L Y S
B U M N E T T I R B U U R N
E J O H N L E N N O N A U H
B O C C H E R I N I L P B O
S T E V I E W O N D E R Y J
```

Solution on Page 333

ACTIVITY	LIFESTYLE
BENEFITS	LIVING
BODY	LONGEVITY
BRAIN	MEDICATION
CARE	MENTAL
CHILDREN	NUTRITION
CLINIC	ORAL
DIET	PHARMACY
DISEASE	PHYSICAL
EDUCATION	REST
EXERCISE	RISK
FITNESS	SLEEP
FLU	SMOKING
FOOD	STRESS
GENETICS	TREATMENT
HEALTHY	WATER
HYGIENE	WEIGHT
ILLNESS	WELLNESS
LEAN	

```
G N I K O M S N I A R B Y X
P P U Q I L L N E S S O Y N
H L A T N E M U E S S D H O
Y C A M R A H P C I E Y E I
S H I E C I N I L C N M A T
I I F T A C T I V I T Y L A
C L O N G E V I T Y I B T C
A D W Y N I L B O E F R H I
L R A E N F E Y S N E M Y D
E E G G L N O I T A C U D E
S N N A E L C O T S P A S M
T W E F R R N M D T E A R R
R A I I E I E E L F E F M E
E T A X G N S A S S L I I A
S E E Z T Y R K I S S U D L
S R E S T O H D W E I G H T
```

Solution on Page 334

APPETIZER	JULIENNE
BASTE	KNIFE
BLANCH	MINCE
BOIL	OVEN
BURNER	PARE
CHEF	PEPPER
CHOP	POACH
CLARIFY	PUREE
COAT	RECIPE
CODDLE	REDUCE
COMPOTE	SALT
COOL	SCALD
CREAM	SCORE
CUT IN	SEAR
DREDGE	SIMMER
FILLET	SLIVER
FLAKE	STIR
FLUTE	TEASPOON
FORK	TOAST
GRATE	ZEST

```
X Q J O H B P O H C E J U E
B J D L P O K T R C R M K L
F O R K H U B V H E A Z O A
K N I F E F R C O M P O T E
K J B L I K N E L T C R P C
S T L A S A A S E A R E O N
C O D D L E Y L P J R C E I
A A E B Z R L P F V E I X M
L S J U L I E N N E N P F R
D T Y S F T O P R C R E M Y
D V L L I O C O P R U I B F
P R U Z P M C C E E B T T S
S T E S E S M H T D P A I S
E R A D D S L E A U O S P N
N E V O G Z T F R C R E A M
T S L I V E R A G E T S A B
```

Solution on Page 334

BROADLEAF

CEDAR CHIPS

CLIPPING

CRABGRASS

CURB

DANDELIONS

DROP SPREADER

EDGING

EXCAVATION

FENCE

FERTILIZER

FILL

GATE

GRUBS

LAWN MOWER

LEVELING

MANICURE

MANURE

PATIO

PEAT MOSS

PESTICIDE

PLUGS

RAIL

RETAINING WALL

SHRUBS

SOD

ST. AUGUSTINE

THATCH

TIES

TRENCHING

TRIMMING

WEED EATER

WEED KILLER

```
T S G F R E Z I L I T R E F
R M R E F X S G U L P W D I
I A U R H C T A H T E E R L
M N B E B A R S G S A E O L
M U S L R V E O S T T D P D
I R B L U A N D P A M E S C
N E R I C T C A I U O A P L
G W O K R I H N H G S T R I
N O A D A O I D C U S E E P
I M D E B N N E R S H R A P
L N L E G B G L A T R A D I
E W E W R G J I D I U I E N
V A A P A T I O E N B L R G
E L F T S F E N C E S E I T
L C E I S P E S T I C I D E
M A N I C U R E D G I N G K
```

Solution on Page 334

ALCOTT	HANCOCK
ALI	HEARST
ANTHONY	HOOVER
ARMSTRONG	JACKSON
BELL	JEFFERSON
CHAPLIN	KELLER
COLUMBUS	KENNEDY
DISNEY	KING
EDISON	LEWIS AND CLARK
EINSTEIN	LINCOLN
FITZGERALD	MONROE
FORD	PARKS
FRANKLIN	TUBMAN
FROST	WASHINGTON
GATES	WINFREY

Movers and Shakers

```
J N U G H W N A M B U T D J
M B D N Q O A V E K L L S E
L E W I S A N D C L A R K M
P A R K S I X O D R L I Y O
W P C N Q N C X E K C N D N
C A C K L N E G H O O V E R
J O S R A O Z Y F H T J N O
H A L H L T C W T O T A N E
L R L U I T I N T S R A E H
R P E F M N A I I M O D K L
M I B L F B G E S L I R B V
R U F R L H U T E S P G F F
Z J E F F E R S O N W A H O
J Y P F L O K N E N E T H Z
Z F R A N K L I N V U E L C
J K A G R P J E I D D S C H
```

Solution on Page 334

ACCENT	HYPERBOLE
ALLEGORY	IMAGERY
ALLUSION	IRONY
ANALOGY	LIMERICK
ANECDOTE	LYRIC
AUTHOR	METAPHOR
BALLAD	NARRATOR
BOOKS	NOVELLA
CHARACTER	PLOT
CLIMAX	POETRY
COMEDY	PROSE
CONFLICT	SATIRE
DIALOGUE	SETTING
DICTION	SIMILE
DRAMA	SONNET
EPIC	STANZA
ESSAY	STORY
FABLE	THESIS
GENRE	TRAGEDY
GLOSSARY	

```
T O L P N K C I R E M I L E N
N Y D E M O C Q U S K O O B B
E R I T A S I G N I T T E S
C L I M A X O T C I R Y L R R
C S I M I L E A C I P E P A A
A I S E A L L U S I O N O L L
N M V I R L A M A R D T E L L
A A D G E N A N E C D O T E E
L G F G L B E T V A P C R V
O E O A O O C G L R I O Y O
G R A S B A S L O L H D S N
Y Y U T R L A S F P E T O Y
A X T A E B E N A G O M N N
S N H N P R O T A R R A N O
S C O Z Y C E R Y S Y U E R
E Y R A H M T S I S E H T I
```

Solution on Page 335

AGILITY

ANCHORS

BELAY

BOULDERS

COMPETITIONS

DANGEROUS

DEMANDING

ENDURANCE

EXTREME

FALL

FREE CLIMBING

FREE SOLOING

FUN

GEAR

GYM

HANDHOLD

HARNESS

HEIGHTS

ICE CLIMBING

MOUNTAINEERING

OUTDOORS

PHYSICAL

ROCK WALLS

ROPES

SCRAMBLING

SHOES

SPORTS

STRENGTH

SUMMIT

TECHNIQUES

TRAINING

WEBBING

Rock Climbing

```
N H T G N E R T S H O E S E
Y T R A I N I N G E A R R M
T I M M U S R O O D T U O E
E C N A R U D N E H X U H R
C O M P E T I T I O N S C T
H A R N E S S G F T U F N X
N S U O R E G N A D F R A E
I T G N I B M I L C E E R F
Q R O P E S N B L M S E O D
U O Y A L E B M L Y T S C L
E P E W E B B I N G H O K O
S S C R A M B L I N G L W H
A G I L I T Y C L C I O A D
W N B O U L D E R S E I L N
G I P H Y S I C A L H N L A
S D E M A N D I N G V G S H
```

Solution on Page 335

ACTION	MUSIC
AUDIO	NETFLIX
BACKUP	OPTICAL
BLANK	PAUSE
BLU-RAY	PHILIPS
BURN	PLASTIC
CASE	RECORDABLE
COMPACT	RENTAL
COMPUTER	ROUND
DATA	SCRATCH
DIGITAL	SHOW
DISK	SONY
DRIVE	SPEED
DVD PLAYER	STORAGE
FILM	TECHNOLOGY
FORMAT	TELEVISION
HOME	TOSHIBA
LASER	VHS
MEDIUM	VIDEO
MOVIES	WATCH

```
X T O S H I B A K S I D J M
C Z E G A R O T S E E Q H L
O X H C T A R C S E S M C I
M I G P H I L I P S R U T F
P L H S O N Y S R U Z S A V
A F T A M R O F E C K I W P
C T P R E S A L C C I C C S
T E L E V I S I O N S R A D
K N A L B S L M R G E C S B
M U A C N D P Y D Y Y I E M
E V E C R U L L A C I T P O
D I G I T A L L B R A S N V
I D V E T I P W L O U A R I
U E R N O D O Y E U D L U E
M O E Z V H S N F N I P B S
S R N D S P A T A D O Z O D
```

Solution on Page 335

ANNUALS

ARCHES

BACKGROUND

BARK

BEANS

BEDS

BIENNIAL

BLOOM

BORDER

BRICKS

CARNATIONS

CARROTS

CLIPPERS

COMPOST

DAISY

EGGPLANT

FENCES

FERTILIZER

FOLIAGE

FROST

HERBAL

MARIGOLD

NUTRIENTS

ORCHARD

PATIO

PEAT MOSS

PERENNIALS

POOLS

RASPBERRIES

ROTOTILLER

SPRINKLERS

STEPS

STRAWBERRIES

VINE

WEEDING

```
B A R K D L O G I R A M F T
S P R I N K L E R S T E P S K
K E F C R E Z I L I T R E F
C J I A H S L A U N N A G O
I P E R E N N I A L S S G L
R P C R R E D R O B E P P I
B E A O E E N I V A C B L A
S A T T M L B S X C N E A G
W T S S I P L W L K E R N E
E M N T O O O I A G F R T D
E O A E O R P S T R K I S R
D S E P I P F C T O T E E A
I S B H E R B A L U T S H H
N C A R N A T I O N S O C C
G Y S I A D R U S D E B R R
M O O L B I E N N I A L A O
```

Solution on Page 335

ANDROMEDA	DRACO
AQUILA	ERIDANUS
AURORAS	LACERTA
BLACK HOLES	LUPUS
CAMELOPARDUS	MENSA
CANES VENATICI	MONOCEROS
CANIS MAJOR	OPHIUCHUS
CANIS MINOR	PEGASUS
CASSIOPEIA	SAGITTARIUS
CEPHEUS	SERPENS
CETUS	STARS
COMA BERENICES	URSA MAJOR
CRUX	URSA MINOR
DARK ENERGY	VELA
DEEP FIELD	

```
C M O N O C E R O S M O S S
E A D L E I F P E E D Y U U
R C N V E L A L N R G R D E
I E U E U B O S A R S O R H
D T N P S H A C E T U J A P
A U U A K V O N A S S A P E
N S E C I N E R E B A M O C
U O A R X K S N O F G S L U
S L S A R O R U A V E I E R
B S L A C E R T A T P N M S
A N D R O M E D A C I A A A
L E R O N I M S I N A C C M
I P I X C A S S I O P E I A
U R S U I R A T T I G A S J
Q E N R A S U H C U I H P O
A S L C Q U R S A M I N O R
```

Solution on Page 336

ACACIA

ARBORIST

BANYAN

BRANCHES

BUCKEYE

CHESTNUT

CITRUS

COTTONWOOD

CYPRESS

DECIDUOUS

DOGWOOD

FILBERT

FRUIT

GRAFT

GUM

HAWTHORN

HEMLOCK

HICKORY

IRONWOOD

JUNIPER

LINDEN

MAGNOLIA

MAHOGANY

MEDLAR

NEEDLES

PALMS

PEAR

PINE CONES

PRUNING

REDWOOD

ROSEWOOD

SANDALWOOD

SASSAFRAS

SEQUOIA

TULIP

```
A C A C I A F I L B E R T B
P D G U M A P R U N I N G R
A O R C J Z K C O L M E H A
L G O Y R O K C I H A C D N
M W S P D E C I D U O U S C
S O E R Y A N C I T R U S H
E O W E S H A W T H O R N E
L D O S S E N O C E N I P S
D O O S J U N I P E R K A N
E O D O O W L A D N A S A F
E W I R O N W O O D S Y R R
N D A O M A H O G A N Y Y U
N E D N I L I T F A R G C I
P R M E D L A R B O R I S T
S E Q U O I A I L O N G A M
I T C H E S T N U T U L I P
```

Solution on Page 336

BACTERIA

BEHAVIOR

BIOLOGY

BREEDING

CELLS

CLONE

CODE

DISEASE

DISORDER

DNA

DOMINANT

EVOLUTION

FAMILY

GENOTYPE

HEIGHT

HEREDITY

HUMANS

INHERITED

LAB

LIFE

MEDICINE

MOLECULAR

MUTATIONS

OFFSPRING

ORGANISMS

PARENTS

RECESSIVE

RNA

SCIENTISTS

SEQUENCING

STRUCTURE

STUDY

TRAITS

VARIATION

VIRUSES

```
Y  T  I  D  E  R  E  H  E  G  B  A  L  R
G  E  V  O  L  U  T  I  O  N  K  S  N  E
E  V  I  S  S  E  C  E  R  I  O  L  V  D
N  C  R  T  T  M  O  L  E  C  U  L  A  R
O  O  U  B  N  S  B  M  Y  N  I  E  C  O
T  D  S  A  E  Y  I  U  S  E  N  C  O  S
Y  E  E  C  R  L  O  T  G  U  H  S  R  I
P  V  S  T  A  I  L  A  N  Q  E  T  G  D
E  R  A  E  P  M  O  T  I  E  R  R  A  O
N  T  O  R  N  A  G  I  R  S  I  U  N  M
I  R  N  I  I  F  Y  O  P  A  T  C  I  I
C  A  Q  A  V  A  G  N  S  E  E  T  S  N
I  I  Y  A  X  A  T  S  F  S  D  U  M  A
D  T  H  G  I  E  H  I  F  I  F  R  S  N
E  S  N  A  M  U  H  E  O  D  C  E  A  T
M  G  N  I  D  E  E  R  B  N  L  I  F  E
```

Solution on Page 336

ANTS	HONEY BEE
BEES	HORNTAIL
BEETLE	JUNE BUG
BLACK WIDOW	LADYBUG
BUMBLEBEE	LIGHTNING BUG
BUTTERFLY	MAYFLY
CATERPILLAR	MOSQUITO
CRICKET	MOTH
DRAGONFLY	PRAYING MANTIS
EARWIG	SCORPION
FIREFLY	SILVERFISH
FLEA	SPIDER
FLIES	SWALLOWTAIL
FRUIT FLY	TERMITE
GNAT	TICK
GRASSHOPPER	WASP

```
B E E T L E T I M R E T X P
S P M A Y F L Y A H T O M S
P G R A L L I P R E T A C A
I R W O D I W K C A L B Q W
D A A K H G F R U I T F L Y
E S R Y S H H O R N T A I L
R S K C I T E K C I R C A F
Y H Y L F N O G A R D S T E
L O N H R I G N A T T M W R
F P G O E N G M R N G O O I
R P U N V G B Z A U B S L F
E E B E L B M U B N E Q L L
T R E Y I U Y Y L E T U A I
T M N B S G D C B Y O I W E
U T U E E A R W I G H T S S
B U J E L S C O R P I O N D
```

Solution on Page 336

BACARDI

BAY BREEZE

BLOODY MARY

BLUE HAWAII

CAPE COD

COSMOPOLITAN

DAIQUIRI

GIN AND TONIC

KAMIKAZE

LONG ISLAND

MAI TAI

MARGARITA

MARTINI

MOJITO

MUDSLIDE

PIÑA COLADA

PINK LADY

RUM AND COKE

SAKE BOMB

SCREWDRIVER

SEA BREEZE

TEQUILA SUNRISE

TOM COLLINS

```
T  I  A  T  I  A  M  A  R  T  I  N  I  M
A  E  K  O  C  D  N  A  M  U  R  C  Z  O
D  P  Q  C  A  P  E  C  O  D  N  G  R  J
A  C  S  U  T  B  A  C  A  R  D  I  E  I
L  O  N  G  I  S  L  A  N  D  H  N  V  T
O  E  I  X  R  L  Y  M  I  U  A  A  I  O
C  D  L  B  A  D  A  M  R  T  B  N  R  K
A  I  L  L  G  C  A  S  I  L  A  D  D  A
N  L  O  O  R  N  S  L  U  F  Y  T  W  M
I  S  C  O  A  C  O  E  Q  N  B  O  E  I
P  D  M  D  M  P  H  H  I  E  R  N  R  K
I  U  O  Y  O  A  Q  V  A  F  E  I  C  A
N  M  T  M  W  I  R  C  D  Z  E  C  S  Z
C  J  S  A  K  E  B  O  M  B  Z  P  M  E
W  O  I  R  S  E  A  B  R  E  E  Z  E  X
C  I  R  Y  D  A  L  K  N  I  P  D  X  T
```

Solution on Page 337

ABIGAIL	JULIA
ANNA	LAURA
BARBARA	LETITIA
BETTY	LOU
CAROLINE	LOUISA
CLAUDIA	LUCRETIA
DOLLEY	LUCY
EDITH	MAMIE
ELEANOR	MARGARET
ELIZABETH	MARTHA
FLORENCE	MARY
FRANCES	MICHELLE
GRACE	NANCY
HARRIET	PATRICIA
HELEN	RACHEL
HILLARY	ROSALYNN
IDA	SARAH
JACKIE	THELMA
JANE	

```
Z F H P J N G Z Z Y H U T C
M A S L A U R A H T R A M E
J R P L N N A Y T H L A I S
H F B O E J C L E E W M M A
J T A U M T E N B L A I I R
F X R I F H I D A M L D R A
R H B S C L H T Z A U O L H
A L A A O I O Y I A N N D W
N P R R J E R R L A I L U J
C N A I R A L C E Y C U L L
E C Y T L I C L B N V C N K
S D W L R D E K E E C R A M
A B I G A I L T I H T E N C
N H D T I S C U M E C T C F
N E L E H W O I C D X I Y Q
A Y T T M T E R A G R A M D
```

Solution on Page 337

BEEF JERKY

CANDY BAR

CANDY CANE

CARAMEL

CHEESE CURLS

CHIPS

CHOCOLATE

COOKIES

CRACKERS

DOUGHNUT

DRIED FRUIT

FRENCH FRIES

GRANOLA

GUMMY BEARS

ICE CREAM

JELLY BEANS

LICORICE

LOLLIPOP

NACHOS

ONION RINGS

PEANUTS

PISTACHIOS

POPCORN

PRETZELS

TAFFY

TRAIL MIX

Late-Night Snacks

```
Y  G  R  A  N  O  L  A  S  O  H  C  A  N
P  F  U  E  N  E  N  A  C  Y  D  N  A  C
S  E  F  M  G  M  G  A  K  I  I  I  H  L
A  Q  A  A  M  A  E  R  C  E  C  I  E  O
O  B  D  N  T  Y  E  Y  C  H  P  M  T  B
N  S  D  D  U  J  B  H  E  S  A  F  A  D
I  N  R  H  F  T  R  E  B  R  E  X  L  V
O  A  I  E  P  I  S  T  A  C  H  I  O  S
N  E  E  S  R  E  K  C  A  R  C  M  C  L
R  B  D  X  C  O  O  K  I  E  S  L  O  I
I  Y  F  U  P  O  P  C  O  R  N  I  H  C
N  L  R  A  B  Y  D  N  A  C  Y  A  C  O
G  L  U  J  I  S  L  E  Z  T  E  R  P  R
S  E  I  R  F  H  C  N  E  R  F  T  J  I
N  J  T  U  N  H  G  U  O  D  G  D  J  C
C  F  P  O  P  I  L  L  O  L  V  K  A  E
```

Solution on Page 337

ACROBATICS

APPLES

AUDIENCE

BALLS

BEANBAGS

CATCHING

CHAINSAWS

CIRCUS

CLOWN

CLUBS

FESTIVAL

FIRE

HANDS

HOBBY

JESTER

JUGGLERS

KNIVES

MOTION

OBJECTS

PERFORMER

PROP

RHYTHM

RINGS

SHOW

SKILL

SPORTS

THROWING

TORCHES

TOSS

TRICKS

Juggling

```
Y  N  R  S  C  I  T  A  B  O  R  C  A  G
P  N  X  S  G  H  R  A  S  E  V  I  N  K
R  P  C  E  H  U  A  B  W  S  K  I  L  L
L  E  F  H  O  O  C  I  Q  X  W  M  L  M
P  I  M  C  P  G  W  I  N  O  N  P  A  Z
H  Y  O  R  C  M  N  X  R  S  I  X  V  D
V  A  O  O  O  A  J  H  I  C  A  G  I  S
B  P  P  T  A  F  T  F  V  Z  U  W  T  T
R  U  I  P  J  C  R  C  I  I  D  S  S  C
I  O  O  Q  L  U  R  E  H  R  I  A  E  E
N  G  K  O  S  E  G  D  P  I  E  F  F  J
G  X  W  L  T  M  S  G  A  B  N  A  E  B
S  N  L  S  R  S  B  U  L  C  C  G  U  O
X  A  E  H  O  B  B  Y  X  E  E  R  P  Q
B  J  I  T  P  M  H  T  Y  H  R  R  T  D
H  A  N  D  S  V  T  R  I  C  K  S  A  T
```

Solution on Page 337

ADDICTION	HEADACHE
ALERTNESS	HEART RATE
ALKALOID	HYPER
AWAKE	JITTERS
BEANS	JOLT
BITTER	KOLA NUT
BUZZ	LATTE
CAPPUCCINO	LEAVES
CHEMICAL	MOLECULE
CHOCOLATE	PILLS
COCA COLA	PLANT
COFFEE	POP
CUP	RED BULL
DECAF	SLEEP
DIURETIC	SODA
DRINKS	SOFT DRINK
DRUG	STIMULANT
ENERGY	TEA
ESPRESSO	WITHDRAWAL
FRUIT	

```
I C O N I C C U P P A C A V
Z I S L L I P L A N T L O J
Z T R E T T I B E N E R G Y
U E E T E S S E N T R E L A
B R T N S N O I T C I D D A
K U T A P D F D Q L M B R S
W I I L R E T E A A O U I L
U D J U E T D B J W L L N E
H E G M S A R E C A E L K E
E C A I S L I A H R C E S P
A A W T O O N N E D U A V L
D F A S P C K S M H L V F A
A L K A L O I D I T E E R T
C R E P Y H P G C I H S U T
H C O C A C O L A W Q G I E
E E F F O C K O L A N U T P
```

Solution on Page 338

APERTURE	LENS
ASPECT	LIGHT
CAMERA	MEGAPIXEL
CANON	MEMORY
CAPTURE	OLYMPUS
CARD	PICTURES
COMPUTERS	PIXELS
CROPPING	PRINTING
DELETE	RAW
DOWNLOAD	SCANNING
EASY	SENSOR
EDITING	SHARE
EXPOSURE	SIZING
FILTER	SLR
FLASH	SOFTWARE
FOCUS	SONY
IMAGING	STORAGE
INTERNET	UPLOAD
KODAK	VIEW
LANDSCAPE	ZOOM

Digital Photography

```
Y N O S F T E N R E T N I R
Q S F I L T E R X L E N S O
W S A M A R D P A F O C U S
C C W E S M O O Z W E I V N
R A W M H S W C A P T U R E
W N J O U I N G C C T F P S
P N H R C K L R S C A N O N
G I E Y O B O O L Y M P U S
W N C D M P A P E R T U R E
I G A T P P D E X G E S G E
T K A I U P P R I N T I N G
H C N R T R W A P I E Z I A
G G E D E U E H A T L I G R
I W R P R M H S G I E N A O
L A N D S C A P E D D G M T
C U P L O A D C M E I Y I S
```

Solution on Page 338

ABYSSINIAN	MEOW
ALLEY	MOUSE
ATTITUDE	NEUTER
BOMBAY	NINE LIVES
CALICO	PANTHER
CARNIVOROUS	PERSIAN
CAT FOOD	POUND
COLLAR	PURRING
CUTE	RUSSIAN BLUE
DOMESTICATED	SIAMESE
EARS	SOFT
FELINE	SPAY
FERAL	STALK
FLEAS	STRETCH
FRIENDLY	TABBY
HAVANA BROWN	TIGER
HISSING	VET
LEOPARD	WITCHES
MAINE COON	YARN

```
P O U N D Y C O L L A R E F
M O U S E A V P U R R I N G
H Y O L L U E J B O M B A Y
C F L I C A T F O O D D I F
T A C S A X R E G I T O S E
E O A S R Y U D R O N M R L
R D B E N L S U H C I E E I
T Y Y H I D S T I L N S P N
S B S C V N I I S E E T A E
A B S T O E A T S O L I N S
E A I I R I N T I P I C T E
L T N W O R B A N A V A H M
F A I E U F L V G R E T E A
K L A T S C U T E D S E R I
N R N O O C E N I A M D L S
S W O E M Y A P S Y A R N D
```

Solution on Page 338

ART MUSEUM

BENTON PARK

BLUES

BOTANICAL GARDEN

BREWERY

CARDINALS

DUTCHTOWN SOUTH

EADS BRIDGE

FOREST PARK

GATEWAY ARCH

GRAND CENTER

HISTORY MUSEUM

LAFAYETTE SQUARE

LASALLE PARK

LEMP MANSION

MAGIC HOUSE

MISSOURI

RAMS

SCIENCE CENTER

SHAW

TOWER GROVE

UNION STATION

ZOO

```
B T B G R A N D C E N T E R R
R M O L A S A L L E P A R K
E A T B L U E S U O S H A W
W G A T E W A Y A R C H U M E
E I N G M B D T U E A M Q U R
R C I K P E S O N T R U S E Y
Y H C R M N B W I N D E E S
M O A A A T R E O E I S T U
I U L P N O I R N C N U T M
S S G T S N D G S E A M E Y
S E A S I P G R T C L T Y R
O O R E O A E O A N S R A O
U U D R N R M V T E G A F T
R U E O G K S E I I H M A S
I I N F C C Z O O C T S L I
D U T C H T O W N S O U T H
```

Solution on Page 338

ALIGNED

ASTRONOMY

ATMOSPHERE

BLOCK

CELESTIAL

CYCLE

DARKNESS

EARTH

ECLIPSE

EVENT

FULL MOON

HORIZON

NASA

NIGHT

OBSERVE

OMEN

ORBIT

PARTIAL

PASSES

PENUMBRAL

RARE

RAYS

REFRACTION

SCIENCE

SHADOW

SKY

SOLAR

SPACE

SUNLIGHT

TELESCOPE

TOTALITY

VIEWING

VISIBLE

```
E L B I S I V P T N H Z Z N
C A V K R J F V D H W Z E Y
N A S A Z Q Q Q R S G M V Z
E U P E S P I L C E O I E U
I B P O S S E N K R A D N H
C L L N E S U N L I G H T E
S A N O O M L L U F U R N P
R I O Z C Y C L E M A M T O
P T I I W K R A R E B A O C
A S T R O N O M Y R K R T S
S E C O D N D E N G I L A E
S L A H A B P A R T I A L L
E E R E H P S O M T A I I E
S C F A S V I E W I N G T T
K L E V R E S B O R R A Y S
Y O R B I T E C A P S K N L
```

Solution on Page 339

APPLICATION

BAD DEBT

BANK ONE

BORROW

CITICORP

COLLATERAL

CREDIT CARD

CREDIT UNION

CURRENT ASSET

DEBIT CARD

DEFAULT

DELINQUENT

DRIVE-THROUGH

FEES

FIRST NATIONAL

FIRST UNION

FUNDS

INTERNET

J.P. MORGAN

MUTUAL FUND

NET WORTH

RATIO

RECOURSE

RISK

SAVINGS

TERM

TREASURY BILLS

WELLS FARGO

```
S M U N O I N U T S R I F B
E U D D B A D D E B T I O O
E T E S S A T N E R R U C R
F U B R E C O U R S E N B R
I A I N H N C I T X A S H O
O L T N O E O N T G S G T W
G F C E F I A K R A U N L C
R U A T N T T O N O R I U O
A N R W I R M A R A Y V A L
F D D O M P E H C Y B A F L
S S N R J X T T J I I S E A
L A E T N E U Q N I L E D T
L T Y H V R I S K I L P A E
E U C I T I C O R P S E P R
W C R E D I T U N I O N L A
C D R A C T I D E R C K I L
```

Solution on Page 339

ANACONDA

ANTEATER

APES

BEES

BINTURONG

CAIMAN

CASSOWARY

CATERPILLAR

CHAMELEONS

CHIMPANZEES

COATI

COBRA

COYPU

CROCODILES

HARPY EAGLE

HOWLER MONKEY

KAKAPO

KOMODO DRAGON

LEAF CANOPY

LEMUR

OCELOT

OKAPIS

ORANGUTANS

PARROTS

PEACOCKS

PORCUPINES

PROTECTED

TEMPERATE

UNDERGROWTH

VIPERS

Rainforests

```
S N O E L E M A H C O Y P U
N E C N F D E T C E T O R P
A P E S B A N A C O N D A O
T X L Z I U O R R I N H K R
U Z O H N R K B O T A O E C
G H T H T A A O C A M W T U
N T L A U L P C O O I L A P
A W E R R L I M D C A E R I
R O A P O I S O I Q C R E N
O R F Y N P D E L H M M P E
P G C E G R U M E L C O M S
A R A A A A E N I S B Q N E R
K E N G S T O R R A P K T E
A D O L C A N T E A T E R P
K N P E A C O C K S R Y R I
N U Y R A W O S S A C D D V
```

Solution on Page 339

ACCUSE	INNOCENT
ACQUIT	JUDGE JUDY
ALLY MCBEAL	JUDGING AMY
ARRAIGN	L.A. LAW
BAIL	LIBEL
BOSTON LEGAL	NIGHT COURT
BRIEF	NO CONTEST
CITE	PEOPLE'S COURT
CRIMINAL	PERRY MASON
DEFENDANT	PLEA
DIVORCE COURT	POLYGRAPH
FAMILY LAW	PRO BONO
GRIEVANCE	RECUSE
HABEAS CORPUS	SEARCH WARRANT
HUNG JURY	

```
L G R I E V A N C E T I C I
I H P D W N O C O N T E S T
B U T R U O C S E L P O E P
E N Y M A G N I G D U J A T
L G S P O L Y G R A P H R N
P J P U L A L A W T F U C A
E U R B P A Y Y R A O E H D
R R O R A R N U M C N S W N
R Y B I M I O I E C F U A E
Y A O E D C L C M D B C R F
M C N F T Y R P S I Z E R E
A Q O H L O N G I A R R A D
S U G A V A C C U S E C N L
O I W I N N O C E N T B T R
N T D B O S T O N L E G A L
Y D U J E G D U J P L E A H
```

Solution on Page 339

AHI TUNA

ALBACORE

BLOWFISH

CALIFORNIA ROLL

CHOPSTICKS

CLAMS

CRAB

CUCUMBER

EEL

EGGPLANT

FISH EGGS

HALIBUT

HAND ROLL

LOBSTER

MISO SOUP

OCTOPUS

OYSTERS

RICE

SALMON

SASHIMI

SCALLOPS

SEAWEED

SESAME SEEDS

SHRIMP

SOY SAUCE

SOYBEANS

SQUID

SWORDFISH

TOFU

TROUT

WRAP

YELLOWTAIL

```
I T U O R T C B N P A C R A M
M K C K R H A L I B U T I Z I
I L O P I R O F O C M A C L L
H S K O C T O P U S N M L I I
S C G Y E N O M L A S O A A A
A A Q G A L B A C O R E M T S
S L S D E E S E M A S E S W N
N L R I R H C H I K W U E O A
A O E U A U S N C X O S G L E
E P T Q A I R I T R R H G L B
B S S F O T O F E D R P E Y
Y E Y W F S F N R T F I L Y O
O O O I P U O S O S I M A W S
S L L O R D N A H B S P N R B
B A H I T U N A N O H D T A C
C C S E A W E E D L U L C P
```

Solution on Page 340

ACTIVITIES

ART

AUDITORIUM

BUILDING

BUSES

CAFETERIA

CHILDREN

CLASSROOMS

COLLEGE

COMPUTERS

CURRICULUM

EDUCATION

ELEMENTARY

ENGLISH

EXAM

GRADUATE

GYM

LEARNING

MATH

MIDDLE

MUSIC

PAPER

PEN

PLAYGROUND

PRESCHOOL

READING

SCIENCE

SECONDARY

STUDENTS

TEACHERS

TESTS

TEXTBOOKS

UNIVERSITY

Going to School

```
Y T E X T B O O K S G Y M H
O Y E L S T U D E N T S U S
P T C O L L E G E M V C S I
E I N O I T A C U D E O I L
N S E H T A M L S S Y M C G
E R I C G S U A D E R P A N
R E C S N C P S Y I A U F E
D V S E I B L S R T D T E T
L I G R N U A R A I N E T E
I N R P R I Y O T V O R E A
H U A A A L G O N I C S R C
C T D P E D R M E T E T I H
E E U E L I O S M C S X A E
X S A R U N U G E A A M G R
A T T M Y G N E L D D I M S
M S E S U B D R E A D I N G
```

Solution on Page 340

BELL	HOOK
BLEEDER	JAB
BLOCKING	KNOCK OUT
BOUT	LIGHTWEIGHT
BOXER HANDSHAKE	MANAGER
BRAWLER	MOUTHPIECE
CLINCH	PROMOTER
COMBINATION	PUNCH
CORNERS	REFEREE
COUNT	RINGSIDE
CUTMAN	ROPE-A-DOPE
DOWN	ROPES
DRAW	ROUNDS
FOOTWORK	SOUTHPAW
FOUL	UPPER CUT
GLOVES	WARNING
HEAVYWEIGHT	WEAVING

```
R E D E E L B O U T S C B D
D O W N K Z E E R E F E R T
Q B P Z A N D K R K Z A H G
R L A E H I O E O N W G M N
E O W J S C G C C O I L O I
L C P G D A N W K E H I U N
W K N E N M A I W O T G T R
A I A A A P F Y L A U H H A
R N M P H D V O N C C T P W
B G T T R A O I U N R W I C
W L U O E O B P U L E E E O
C O C H X M M P E X P I C U
S V F O O T W O R K P G E N
K E O C B E L L T Q U H R T
P S X A G N I V A E W T L T
I R O U N D S R E N R O C T
```

Solution on Page 340

ALGEBRA BOOK	LOCKER
BACKPACK	MARKER
BINDER	MATH BOOK
CALCULATOR	PAPER
COMPASS	PEN
DICTIONARY	PENCIL
ENGLISH BOOK	PROTRACTOR
ERASER	RULER
FOLDER	SCIENCE BOOK
GYM CLOTHES	SPANISH BOOK
HIGHLIGHTER	STAPLER
HISTORY BOOK	STUDENT ID
LIBRARY CARD	THESAURUS

```
H  B  A  R  O  T  C  A  R  T  O  R  P  P
I  A  D  R  E  K  R  A  M  K  V  E  A  W
S  C  I  E  N  C  E  B  O  O  K  T  P  Z
T  K  T  S  G  Y  M  C  L  O  T  H  E  S
O  P  N  U  L  L  S  L  O  B  R  G  R  K
R  A  E  R  I  I  S  B  C  H  E  I  U  O
Y  C  D  U  S  B  A  P  K  S  S  L  L  O
B  K  U  A  H  R  P  V  E  I  A  H  E  B
O  F  T  S  B  A  M  B  R  N  R  G  R  H
O  F  S  E  O  R  O  H  J  A  E  I  P  T
K  O  G  H  O  Y  C  N  M  P  L  H  E  A
L  L  Y  T  K  C  F  L  Z  S  P  E  N  M
A  D  R  O  T  A  L  U  C  L  A  C  C  V
L  E  B  E  Y  R  A  N  O  I  T  C  I  D
D  R  W  R  E  D  N  I  B  Y  S  G  L  E
T  Z  U  B  E  C  N  V  U  F  S  O  S  F
```

Solution on Page 340

AMPLIFIER	ENGINEER
ANALOG	HARDWARE
APPLIANCES	MEMORY
BIT	MICROCHIP
BOARD	MODERN
CAPACITORS	PASSIVE
CIRCUIT	POWER
COMPLEX	PROCESSOR
COMPONENTS	RAM
COMPUTERS	RESISTOR
CONDUCTOR	SILICON
CORE	SOLDER
DESIGN	SUBSTRATE
DEVICE	TECHNOLOGY
DIGITAL	TRANSISTOR
ELECTRONIC	VLSI
ELEMENTS	WIRE

```
R J M A R O T S I S I S N A R T
O R E D L O S C O M P L E X
T I U C R I C S W P B R J P
C E R O C A M P L I F I E R U
U E C A P A C I T O R S T O
D L L H A N A L O G E T A C
N E A E N N W R D M E N R E
O M V T C O O O E E N E T S
C E L E I T L W S M I N S S
I N S A S G R O I O G O B O
L T I I Z A I O G R N P U R
I S S B O A R D N Y E M S E
S E P I H C O R C I M O K W
R N S R E T U P M O C C T O
H A R D W A R E V I S S A P
C Q E C I V E D N R E D O M
```

Solution on Page 341

AMERICIUM	LAWRENCIUM
ANTIMONY	MANGANESE
ARSENIC	MENDELEVIUM
BERKELIUM	NEODYMIUM
CADMIUM	OSMIUM
CERIUM	PRASEODYMIUM
CESIUM	PROTACTINIUM
COBALT	RHENIUM
EINSTEINIUM	RUTHENIUM
EUROPIUM	STRONTIUM
GADOLINIUM	TECHNETIUM
GERMANIUM	TELLURIUM
IODINE	XENON
LANTHANUM	ZINC

```
M T E M A N G A N E S E P Q
U E U E M M U I T N O R T S
I C R I E K C C O B A L T G
N H O N R C I N E S R A N A
E N P S I Q M C E S I U M D
H E I T C Y N O M I T N A O
R T U E I O D M U I R E C L
U I M I U Y M U I M D A C I
T U Q N M M U I M Y D O E N
H M U I N I T C A T O R P I
E F U U M U I N A M R E G U
N M X M E N D E L E V I U M
I U E Z G B E R K E L I U M
U E N I D O I W M U I M S O
M Q O N M U N A H T N A L A
X Z N C T E L L U R I U M S
```

Solution on Page 341

ADDAMS FAMILY

ANDY GRIFFITH

BEWITCHED

BONANZA

DICK VAN DYKE

DRAGNET

FLYING NUN

GET SMART

GIDGET

GILLIGAN'S ISLAND

GUNSMOKE

HOGAN'S HEROES

HONEYMOONERS

I LOVE LUCY

LASSIE

LEAVE IT TO BEAVER

MCHALE'S NAVY

MISTER ED

MUNSTERS

MY THREE SONS

RAWHIDE

TWILIGHT ZONE

```
S D R Y E I S S A L V N G G
J N E V X I L O V E L U C Y
J A V A Z N A N O B I M L U
G L A N D Y G R I F F I T H
I S E S I G G S K D M S W O
D I B E C E U N Y A U T I G
G S O L K T N O F D N E L A
E N T A V S S L E S R I N
T A T H A M M E Y H T E G S
E G I C N A O E I C E D H H
N I E M D R K R N T R I T E
G L V D Y T E H G I S H Z R
A L A H K Q S T N W S W O O
R I E Y E T S Y U E B A N E
D G L O T C K M N B X R E S
Q S R E N O O M Y E N O H O
```

Solution on Page 341

CINDERELLA

DAISY DUCK

DONALD DUCK

DUMBO

FRONTIERLAND

GOOFY

HAUNTED MANSION

INDIANA JONES RIDE

MAIN STREET

MATTERHORN

MICKEY MOUSE

MINNIE MOUSE

PETER PAN

PIRATES

PLUTO

SLEEPING BEAUTY

SMALL WORLD

SNOW WHITE

SPACE MOUNTAIN

SPLASH MOUNTAIN

STAR TOURS

TINKER BELL

Disneyland

```
G V T I N K E R B E L L V S
Q N D N A L R E I T N O R F
H I S D O N A L D D U C K I
Y A R I K C U D Y S I A D E
Y T U A E B G N I P E E L S
N N O N E T C H U A Y S R U
R U T A T E I U X C F U O O
O O R J I E N O S E O O W M
H M A O H R D B E M O M L E
R H T N W T E M T O G Y L I
E S S E W S R U A U S E A N
T A O S O N E D R N I K M N
T L T R N I L D I T S C S I
A P U I S A L C P A W I B M
M S L D C M A D K I A M O E
V G P E T E R P A N O M V N
```

Solution on Page 341

PUZZLES • 117

AUTOMATION

BLENDER

CAMCORDER

CAMERAS

CLEANING

CLOCKS

COMPACTOR

COOKING

DEVICES

DISHWASHER

DOMESTIC

DRYER

ELECTRICAL

FREEZER

HEATER

HOUSEHOLD

IRON

KITCHEN

LOAD

MACHINES

MAJOR

MECHANICAL

MICROWAVE

MIXER

OVENS

RANGE

REPAIR

SERVICE

SMALL

STOVE

TECHNOLOGY

TELEPHONE

TOASTER

WASHING

```
S D A O L A C I N A H C E M
S K C O L C S T O V E N S G
G N I N A E L C I H D Y Y N
N N E H C T I K T R L G R I
I R E X I M U M A J O R E K
H F X R R R S N M L H U T O
S R B E T E G Z O L E E A O
A E M T C E H N T A S C E C
W E I S E A H S U M U I H I
R Z C A L C M S A S O V D T
E E R O E J K C E W H R N S
P R O T C A P M O C H E O E
A N W B L E N D E R I S R M
I S A R E M A C F P D V I O
R Q V T E L E P H O N E E D
X S E N I H C A M R E Y R D
```

Solution on Page 342

ANGST

ANNOYANCE

ANTICIPATION

APPREHENSION

AWE

DELIGHT

DESIRE

DISCONTENTMENT

EMBARRASSMENT

ENVY

EUPHORIA

FRIENDSHIP

GLADNESS

GLEE

HOMESICKNESS

HOPE

HUMILITY

HYPOCRISY

IMPATIENCE

JEALOUSY

KINDNESS

LONELINESS

LUST

NERVOUSNESS

PAIN

PHOBIA

REPENTANCE

RESENTMENT

SURPRISE

TERROR

```
K T I E C N A T N E P E R T
T N E M T N E T N O C S I D
D E U B X K G Y N F H O P E
E M P A S I S S R L U J N L
S T H R S N S I I U M O E I
I N O R E D E R M S I E R G
R E R A N N N C P T L S V H
E S I S D E K O A G I S O T
S E A S A S C P T J T E U E
I R H M L S I Y I E Y N S R
R I E E G C S H E A P I N R
P A I N I H E Y N L H L E O
R H X T W R M V C O O E S R
U A N G S T O N E U B N S A
S A P P R E H E N S I O N W
A N N O Y A N C E Y A L U E
```

Solution on Page 342

BAKEWARE

BOWL

BRUSH

CLEANING

CLEAVER

COLANDER

COOKBOOK

COOKING

COPPER

CUTLERY

DRAWER

EATING

FLATWARE

FOOD

FORKS

FRYING PAN

GLASSWARE

GRATER

HOLDER

IRON

KNIVES

MORTAR

OVEN

PANS

PEELER

PLATE

POTS

PRESS

SIEVE

SILVERWARE

SKEWER

SPATULA

SPOONS

STOVE

STRAINER

TOOLS

WASH

Kitchen Utensils

```
D I U E V E I S E V I N K K
D R E D E E T M N X N E V O
O O A S O R E D N A L O C O
O N T W A A A R A T R O M B
F O I I E W Q W E V O T S K
P R N B A R E W E K S P E O
Y E G S S E R P I K A T C O
R T H B P V G N I N A E L C
E A B O W L G I S L R B E S
L R F R Y I N G P A N C A K
T G H T U S K G W H O T V R
U A L U T A P S S P C P E O
C K T O O L S U P J V D R F
F L A T W A R E R E L E E P
R M W C L B R S P O O N S N
A S F G M B U T H U K M X U
```

Solution on Page 342

ALGAE	MEDICINE
BIOLOGY	NATURE
BOTANIST	NUTRITION
BRANCH	PLANT LIFE
CELLS	POLLEN
CLASS	RESEARCH
DISEASES	SCIENCE
ECOLOGY	SEEDS
EVOLUTION	SOIL
FLOWERS	SPECIES
FODDER	STEMS
FUNGI	STRUCTURE
GARDENS	STUDY
GENETICS	TAXONOMY
GRASS	TISSUE
GROWTH	VEGETABLES
HERBS	VEGETATION
LATIN	WATER
LEAVES	

Studying Plants

```
E N I C I D E M S F U N G I
S T U D Y B I O L O G Y E O
H T W O R G P S L A T I N E
Q J P P B O P V E W A T E R
J T M A L G A E C A N F T U
S S A L C A N G A O S S I T
D I E U E C N E I C S E C A
E N O I T I R T U N A L S N
E A H F L H U A L U R B R T
S T C Z C L S T D I G A E I
H O R N O M L I O S F T W S
E B A V E Y G O L O C E O S
R R E T A X O N O M Y G L U
B G S S T R U C T U R E F E
S R E D D O F Z L E A V E S
G A R D E N S E I C E P S I
```

Solution on Page 342

AMUSEMENT

CARTOONS

COMEDY

CONTEXT

CULTURE

EMOTION

ENTERTAIN

FARCE

FUNNY

GAGS

HAPPY

HILARIOUS

HUMOR

HYPERBOLE

IMPROV

JOKES

LAUGHING

PUN

SARCASM

SATIRE

SENSE OF

SLAPSTICK

SMILE

SOCIAL

STAND UP

STORY

SURPRISE

TIMING

VERBAL

VISUAL

WIT

```
Z S K C I T S P A L S N L O
T U X S T O R Y N N U F A B
E R I T A S F T V P O N B H
V P O E M O T I O N I A R J
J R F A E A T W F A R C E L
G I O S S N O O T R A C V X
A S N H U M O R T O L I O E
G E L O B R E P Y H I V R G
S R U Y I T W L K V H I P U
T U C X N H S A R C A S M L
A T N E M E S U M A P U I Z
N L A I C O S G S Y P A S J
D U Y J U H O H E M Y L C G
U C O M E D Y I K C I P C F
P N X T X E T N O C U L F Z
V F T I M I N G J D T M E W
```

Solution on Page 343

ALTER	NEEDLEWORK
BACKSTITCH	PATCHWORK
BATTING	PATTERN
BINDING	PIN
BOBBIN	PLEAT
BUTTONHOLE	POCKET
CLOTH	QUILTING
CUT	SCISSORS
DARNING	SEAMSTRESS
DESIGN	SEWING
EMBROIDERY	STITCHES
EYELET	TACK
FABRIC	TAILOR
GATHER	TECHNIQUES
GUSSET	THIMBLE
HEM	THREAD
LINING	TRIM
MACHINE	YARN
MATERIAL	

```
B  X  O  P  O  C  K  E  T  E  S  S  U  G
K  A  L  A  I  R  E  T  A  M  Y  T  N  N
H  R  C  E  L  B  M  I  H  T  E  I  I  I
D  T  O  K  F  A  B  R  I  C  T  T  B  N
A  R  O  W  S  V  R  A  H  T  P  C  B  I
E  Y  E  L  E  T  O  N  A  A  H  H  O  L
R  J  S  T  C  L  I  B  T  E  G  E  B  G
H  M  R  R  L  Q  D  T  M  L  A  S  P  N
T  A  O  A  U  A  E  E  C  O  T  T  L  I
D  C  S  E  R  R  R  P  E  H  H  A  E  W
E  H  S  N  N  I  Y  A  R  N  E  C  A  E
S  I  I  P  A  T  C  H  W  O  R  K  T  S
I  N  C  I  H  C  G  N  I  T  L  I  U  Q
G  E  S  N  S  E  A  M  S  T  R  E  S  S
N  R  O  L  I  A  T  C  Q  U  U  I  U  U
C  Q  L  G  N  I  D  N  I  B  B  C  M  A
```

Solution on Page 343

BET	MSNBC
BLOOMBERG	PAX TV
BLUE'S CLUES	PEYTON PLACE
BRAVO	RCA
CHANNELS	REALITY SHOWS
CIRCUITS	SAILOR MOON
COURT TV	SCI-FI CHANNEL
DAWSON'S CREEK	SCOOBY-DOO
FOOD NETWORK	SURVIVOR
GAME SHOWS	THE SIMPSONS
GREY'S ANATOMY	TNT
HBO	TODAY SHOW
HGTV	TRANSMITTING
JACKASS	TUBE
MONOCHROMATIC	UPN
MOVING IMAGES	

```
G N I T T I M S N A R T T P
G S E G A M I G N I V O M E
R R C N O O M R O L I A S Y
E O E I T S V O B K V T T T
B V O Y F O S T E E T N I O
M I T D S I D A T E G T U N
O V U X Y A C A K R H K C P
O R B P A B N H Y C U M R L
L U E C N P O A A S A O I A
B S R B R A V O T N H J C C
C I T A M O R H C O N O M E
B L U E S C L U E S M E W Q
N A G A M E S H O W S Y L V
S W O H S Y T I L A E R Z S
M B K R O W T E N D O O F Z
H T H E S I M P S O N S A O
```

Solution on Page 343

ALUMINUM	MONEY
BANK	ONE CENT
BRASS	PRESIDENT
BRONZE	PROFILE
CHANGE	ROUND
COINAGE	SAVE
COLLECTOR	SERIES
COPPER	SHIELD
CURRENCY	SMALL
DATE	SPEND
HEADS	STEEL
HISTORY	TAILS
INFLATION	TREASURY
JAR	USA
LIBERTY	VALUE
LINCOLN	WHEAT
MEMORIAL	YEAR
METAL	ZINC
MINT	

Penny

```
T J Z E Q Y B Q E U L A V Y
N P T M T S T L S A D S S Z
E Y R U S A E R T L M U B S
D M E N U B D E E I A R E L
I O L I C R M I N B O R Y I
S N H M O A H T M N I N A A
E E F U I S H N Z E L L U T
R Y U L N S F E S B L O Z A
P Q Y A A G M C A O A C Q E
J P R H G T R E N D M N R H
A R O R E A I N M I S I K W
R O T C E L L O C O Z L V G
X F S Y V P Y C N E R R U C
D I I J A S P E N D J I F I
C L H R S X R O U N D P A H
Q E G N A H C F C S T E E L
```

Solution on Page 343

APRICOT	LEMON
ARUGULA	LENTILS
AVOCADO	LETTUCE
BANANA	MANGO
BEET	OKRA
CABBAGE	ONIONS
CARROTS	ORANGE
CELERY	PAPAYA
CHERRY	PARSNIP
COCONUT	PEANUT
CORN	PLUM
CURRANT	PUMPKIN
DATE	RADISH
FIG	SALAD
GARLIC	SOYBEAN
GINGER	SPINACH
GUAVA	SQUASH
KALE	TOMATO
KUMQUAT	TURNIP
LEEK	YAM

Healthy Foods

```
M U L P T X X C B E T A D W
H T C P U O G W I A L Y B G
K S D E I M C I M L N P R U
E V A C L N P I N S R A P A
E M L U O E R K R G P A N V
L A A T Q C R U I P E J G A
J N S T U S O Y T N A R I Y
Y G N E S Q N N O L N T F A
N O A L T R C K U H U N C P
I R E R O A R G U T T A S A
S A B C R A U Y A M B R P P
J N Y Y R R E H C B Q R I B
K G O D A C O V A C Q U N E
A E S I C B F G Y S W C A E
L E M O N L E N T I L S C T
E O T A M O T R A D I S H M
```

Solution on Page 344

ASPIRIN

BIOMEDICAL

BODY

CLINICS

DIAGNOSIS

DISEASES

DRUGS

EMERGENCY

EXAM

FEVER

FLU

GENETICS

HEALING

HEALTHCARE

HOSPITALS

ILLNESS

INJURY

INSURANCE

LAB

MEDICATION

NECESSARY

NURSES

PAIN

PATHOLOGY

PEDIATRICS

PHARMACY

PHYSICIANS

PREVENTION

RELIEF

RESEARCH

SYMPTOM

TESTS

TREATMENT

```
H C R A E S E R E L I E F B
N N N O I T A C I D E M P A
U Y I P P F E V E R Y O R L
R L D R A H N P A R R T E T
S I F O I T Y C A V U P V I
E X A M B P H S K I J M E D
S S T C P T S O I S N Y N I
E Z L E L E N A L C I S T A
S M L A C I D E M O I B I G
A P E E T N N I M T G A O N
E H N R P I A I A T E Y N O
S D R U G S P R C T A S B S
I I L L N E S S U S R E T I
D H E A L I N G O S S I R S
O G E N E T I C S H N K C T
A P H A R M A C Y C R I T S
```

Solution on Page 344

BOUNDARIES

CELESTIAL

CHARTS

CITY

COUNTY

DIRT

DISTANCE

ELEVATION

EQUATOR

GEOGRAPHIC

GLOBES

GRID

HEMISPHERE

HIGHWAY

INFORMATION

JUNCTIONS

KEY

KILOMETERS

LAKE

MEASURABLE

NAMING

NORTH POLE

PARK

POPULATION

PORT OF ENTRY

PRIME MERIDIAN

PROJECTIONS

RIVER

SHADED

TOLL

TOPOGRAPHIC

TOWN

TRAVEL

Mapmaking

```
O I S N O I T C N U J A I M
C C I H P A R G O P O T H E
I I Y N S H A D E D P F E A
B E H R F L E V A R T R M S
O C Y P T O G L O B E S I U
U N C T A N R J L L O T S R
N A I D I R E M E M I R P A
D T Y G G C G F A N E A H B
A S O T T N H O O T D H E L
R I O I N I I R E T I C R E
I D O D G U T M K G R O E Q
E N I H B H O E A R T O N U
S R W T P L Y C L N A W P A
G A N O I T A L U P O P D T
Y V L K E L E V A T I O N O
C E L E S T I A L R E V I R
```

Solution on Page 344

ABSINTHE	MEAD
ALCOHOL	MIXED
BARLEY	PARTY
BEER	PORT
BOOZE	PROOF
BOTTLE	PUB
BOURBON	RUM
BRANDY	SCHNAPPS
CHAMPAGNE	SCOTCH
COGNAC	SHERRY
DRINKING	SHOTS
ETHANOL	SPIRITS
GIN	TEQUILA
GLASS	VERMOUTH
HOPS	VODKA
LAGER	WHISKEY
LIQUOR	WINE

```
M A W N J N L R J B Q Q G P
U K S H R B O T T L E E W Z
E D H P I V H B T D E X I M
F O O R P S P I R I T S S U
P V P Z E A K I Y U J C W R
H U S E A E N E F D O I Z G
H C V H T K B H Y T N B L Y
T B A T I H Y R C E J A R P
U J B N L O A H A S S R R U
O Y G I G O L N K S E L O B
M V I S T O H S O H M E U O
R L N B P E C O S L B Y Q O
E N G A P M A H C A H Q I Z
V R R O T E Q U I L A D L E
Q T R O P A O R E G A L U A
Y T Y D B D J X A M J Q D Z
```

Solution on Page 344

BALLROOM	MAMBO
BEAT	MINUET
CANCAN	MODERN
CLOGGING	MOTION
CONTEST	MUSIC
COUNTRY	PARTNER
CULTURE	POLKA
DANCERS	REEL
DISCO	RHYTHM
FANDANGO	RUMBA
FLAMENCO	SALSA
FORMAL	SAMBA
FOXTROT	SHIMMY
HIP-HOP	SHUFFLE
HULA	SOCIAL
JAZZ	SQUARE
JIVE	SWING
LEAD	TANGO
LIMBO	TWIST
LINE	WALTZ

Dance Time

```
S L V P E N I L E E R H Z G
O J X O C N E M A L F Z N M
J B I H K A P O L K A I O F
I E M P D F P O Y J G T R O
V A V I O U M R M G I J O X
E T B H L G T L O O G N A T
R N W M U N N L N Q D D S R
A M N I U L C A X Z T E P O
U A A O S R A B D A T A R T
Q M C U L T U R E N R L W N
S B N Z H L I B O T A S A T
A O A V S R E C N A D F E W
L B C I S U M E L F F U H S
S W M S F O R M A L N P C W
A V L A I C O S H I M M Y X
G N I W S D P V M H T Y H R
```

Solution on Page 345

ACORN

ALMONDS

BARLEY

BRAZIL NUT

BREADNUT

BUCKWHEAT

CASHEW

CEREALS

CHESTNUT

CHICKPEAS

COWPEAS

FLAX

FRUITS

GRAINS

HAZELNUT

HEMP

LEGUMES

LENTILS

MACADAMIA

MAIZE

MILLET

OATS

PEANUTS

PINE NUTS

PUMPKIN

QUINOA

RYE

SEEDS

SOYBEANS

SPELT

SUNFLOWER

WALNUT

WILD RICE

Edible Seeds

```
T S P E L T N V T E L L I M
I W D E T U N T S E H C A R
T E I E A T U N L A W C F E
E H B L E N T I L S A O R W
S S J R D S U S E D C W U O
N A B A A R Z T A Z F P I L
A C E C H Z I M S N I E T F
E R F O C H I C K P E A S N
B S L R P A G L E I H S M U
Y N A N N M P I N E N U T S
O I X H A Z E L N U T K D E
S A B U C K W H E A T N N M
N R T E Y E Q U I N O A S U
R G B S Y N I K P M U P D G
J K B C E R E A L S Q Q S E
T F D K S N B A R L E Y N L
```

Solution on Page 345

ARTIFACTS	HUMANITY
BEHAVIOR	KINSHIP
BIOLOGICAL	LANGUAGES
COUNTRIES	LINGUISTIC
CULTURES	NATURE
DIG	ORIGINS
ECOLOGY	PEOPLE
ETHNICITY	PHILOSOPHY
ETHNOLOGY	PHYSICAL
EVOLUTION	RACE
FAMILY	RELIGION
FOSSIL	RESEARCH
GENEALOGY	SCIENCE
GENETICS	SOCIOLOGY
GROUPS	STUDY
HISTORY	TOOLS

```
W Y G O L O C E C N E I C S
A G E N E T I C S P U O R G
I R E L I G I O N T O O L S
W S N N S E G A U G N A L A
C E O P E T H N I C I T Y K
A I I C H A C U L T U R E S
H R T P I I L A C I S Y H P
U T U S E O L O F A M I L Y
M N L B I O L O G I C A L D
A U O C O U P O S Y T H G U
N O V Q D I G L G O I R L T
I C E R U T A N E Y P R A S
T S N I G I R O I V A H E B
Y R A C E T H N O L O G Y P
R E S E A R C H I S T O R Y
D P I H S N I K F O S S I L
```

Solution on Page 345

CLEARING

DAY HIKE

EIGER

FERNS

FLYING FOX

GIBBON

GRAND TETONS

GROVE

IMPENETRABLE

JAGUARS

MACHETE

MAROON BELLS

MEADOWS

MOUNT MCKINLEY

MOUNTAIN GOAT

MT. EVEREST

MUDSLIDE

OAK TREE

OCELOTS

RAIN GEAR

RAIN JACKET

RAPPEL

SLOTH

THUNDERSTORMS

TREK

VINSON MASSIF

WOODPECKERS

Outdoor Adventure

```
W M A R O O N B E L L S X V
R E L B A R T E N E P M I S
W P M J A G U A R S O U E M
Z O N O B B I G A N A D X R
F O O R U Z Z A P O K S O O
E I E D A N Y Q P T T L F T
R S S T P E T G E E R I G S
N A L S E E G A L T E D N R
S L I O A H C N I D E E I E
M O U N T M C K I N L E Y D
T R E K J H N A E A G V L N
E K I H Y A D O M R R O F U
Y S T O L E C O S G S R A H
S W O D A E M K Y N V G U T
G N I R A E L C E E I G E R
I M T E V E R E S T A V L E
```

Solution on Page 345

ANIMAL	MEDUSOZOA
AQUARIUMS	NATURE
AURELIA	OCEAN
BEACH	ORGANISM
BLOOMS	PAINFUL
CLEAR	POISON
COLORFUL	RED
CUBOZOA	SCYPHOZOA
CURRENTS	SMALL
DEADLY	SOFT
DEEP SEA	STAUROZOA
FIRST AID	STINGING
FISH	SWARMS
FLOATING	SWIMMING
FOOD	TENTACLES
FRESHWATER	TOXIC
GELATINOUS	UMBRELLA
JELLIES	VINEGAR

Jellyfish

```
T O X I C F L O A T I N G T
G A D U M B R E L L A M S F
O B L O O M S I N A G R O O
D E R F O P G N I M M I W S
S A I R E F S F N A T U R E
W C G E L A T I N O U S C I
A H D S M U I R A U Q A U L
R P E H C R N S O R A O B L
M A A W L E G T Z A N Z O E
S I D A E L I A O G I O Z J
G N L T A I N I H E M S O N
O F Y E R A G D P N A U A O
C U R R E N T S Y I L D H S
E L U F R O L O C V A E S I
A O Z O R U A T S A F M I O
N X S E L C A T N E T S F P
```

Solution on Page 346

PUZZLES • 151

AUTOMOBILE

BUS

CHARIOT

CONNECTION

DELAY

DEPARTURE

DUNE BUGGY

GLIDER

HORSE

ICE SKATES

MONORAIL

MOPED

MOTOR HOME

MOTORCYCLE

ROLLER SKATES

ROLLERBLADES

ROWBOAT

SKATEBOARD

SNOWMOBILE

STEERING WHEEL

STROLLER

SUBWAY

SUITCASE

TIRE

TROLLEY CAR

UNICYCLE

VAN

WAGON

WHEELCHAIR

WINDSHIELD

Get Around

```
L S N O W M O B I L E D F D
Y E L C Y C R O T O M D T U
A E E S R O H U E D E R M N
L U U H W G N W R P O L O E
E O T B W I S A O L J I T B
D R O O C G O M L X T A O U
I A U Y M B N E L C G R R G
T C C T E O Y I E U L O H G
P L E T R C B N R L I N O Y
E J A S A A N I B E D O M A
N K H R K O P V L E E M E W
S U I T C A S E A E R T E B
C H A R I O T N D N S I S U
H R I A H C L E E H W Q T S
S T R O L L E R S K A T E S
D L E I H S D N I W A G O N
```

Solution on Page 346

AGE	NURSERY
ART FORM	OLD
ARTISTIC	OUTDOOR
BARK	PENJING
CARE	PERENNIAL
CHINESE	PINE
DWARFING	PLANTING
FORMS	POTTED
GARDEN	PRUNING
GRAFTING	SAMURAI
GREEN	SHAPING
GROWTH	SHRUB
HISTORY	SOIL
HOBBY	STYLES
INDOOR	TOOLS
JAPANESE	TREES
JUNIPER	TRIMMING
LEAVES	WATER
MINIATURE	WIRING
NATURE	ZEN

```
S M C H I N E S E N A P A J
E Y G M T R E E S U E O H M
L R G N I N U R P R B Z J K
Y O U A I D L O E S G J U G
T T B T B J W N E E R G N N
S S A U A O N A E R A C I I
C I R R P I N E R Y F C P T
I H K E A C N D P F T M E N
S T S L S R C I T S I T R A
L W L N A Z T G M R N N A L
E O O S M R O F O K G T G P
A R O O U T D O O R Z E E O
V G T I R Y D G A R D E N T
E S N L A N G N I M M I R T
S H A P I N G N I R I W M E
W A T E R H O B B Y J Z M D
```

Solution on Page 346

AOL	KODAK
AVON	LOUIS VUITTON
CISCO	MARATHON OIL
COSTCO	MORGAN STANLEY
DILLARD	NORTHROP
DOW CHEMICAL	PRUDENTIAL
EBAY	RITE AID
EXXON MOBIL	ROLEX
FANNIE MAE	SAMSUNG
FORD MOTOR	STATE FARM
GILLETTE	THE LIMITED
GOLDMAN SACHS	TIME WARNER
GUCCI	TOYS"R"US
IGA	TRAVELOCITY
J.P. MORGAN	WOOLWORTHS
KFC	

Business Names

```
H D E T I M I L E H T S X G
M F H L I O N O H T A R A M
S O P S A M S U N G V L X R
J R R Z K F C I I T O L T A
N D U G L A O S G I N I R F
G M D I A N C V O M S B A E
P O E L C N T U L E H O V T
O T N L I I S I D W T M E A
R O T E M E O T M A R N L T
H R I T E M C T A R O O O S
T I A T H A S O N N W X C U
R T L E C E I N S E L X I R
O E B D W L C C A R O E T S
N A G R O M P J C P O L Y Y
Y I K A D O K C H U W O I O
L D R A L L I D S Q G R G T
```

Solution on Page 346

PUZZLES • **157**

ANIMANIACS	PINK PANTHER
BUGS AND DAFFY	POPEYE
CARE BEARS	RICHIE RICH
CASPER	SCOOBY-DOO
FAMILY GUY	SIMPSONS
FLINTSTONES	SMURFS
GARFIELD	SOUTH PARK
GUMBY	SPEED RACER
HE-MAN	TAZ-MANIA
JETSONS	TOM AND JERRY
KING OF THE HILL	TRANSFORMERS
LOONEY TUNES	YOGI BEAR

Cartoons

```
K S C A R E B E A R S N U C
R I M B Y U G Y L I M A F A
M S N U Y G S E A C S M S S
L C X G R N N P R H E E I P
S O S S O F O O M I N H M E
C O O A R F S P Y E O G P R
A B U N A Q T S R R T A S E
I Y T D E R E H R I S R O C
N D H D B Y J D E C T F N A
A O P A I B T V J H N I S R
M O A F G M E U D O I E X D
I K R F O U I E N G L L T E
N V K Y Y G Y Z A E F D L E
A I N A M Z A T M L S E G P
V P T R A N S F O R M E R S
P P I N K P A N T H E R O M
```

Solution on Page 347

ANGELS	HAPPINESS
CANDLES	MANGER
CANDY CANES	OFFICE PARTY
CELEBRATE	OPENING GIFTS
CHOIR	PRESENTS
COOKIES	REUNION
DECORATIONS	SECRET SANTA
DRINKING	SKATING
FEAST	SLEIGH RIDES
FESTIVE	SNOW
GATHERINGS	STOCKINGS
GIFT EXCHANGE	TRADITIONS
GIFT GIVING	VACATION
GRANDMA'S HOUSE	YULE

Christmastime

```
C F S X W P R E S E N T S J
S O E E G N I K N I R D E S
N G O S N C O E O O E W G S
O I D K T A H L I P G R N E
W F G E I I C U T E A S A N
A T F N C E V Y I N V Z H I
T G M I I O S E D I A S C P
N I A O C T R M A N C T X P
A V N T P E A A R G A O E A
S I G V H S P K T G T C T H
T N E H H E F A S I I K F S
E G R O E A R E R F O I I L
R E U N I O N I A T N N G E
C S E L D N A C N S Y G S G
E T A R B E L E C G T S U N
S E D I R H G I E L S J V A
```

BAKING

BISCUIT

BROWNIES

BUTTER

CHEF

CHIPS

CHOCOLATE

CUTTER

DESSERT

DOUGH

DROP

EGGS

FAT

FLAT

FLOUR

FRUITS

GINGER

GIRL SCOUT

ICING

JAR

MILK

MONSTER

NUTS

OATMEAL

OREO

OVEN

PRESSED

RAISIN

RECIPE

ROUND

SHORTBREAD

SNACK

SOFT

SPICES

SUGAR

SWEET

TREAT

VANILLA

Cookies

```
R H G U O D N U O R L F E Y
U E K E G I R L S C O U T Q
O K C H I P S C H E F H S X
L C W I C H O C O L A T E L
F R U T P E E P R J E I I Z
Q B U T T E R B T Y G U N N
S W E E T E O R B N G C W X
O P M X S E E V R H S S O U
F O F S A S R J E T P I R S
R R E T S N O M A N I B B U
C D A E R S A F D R C A S G
A L D E T I T F O S E K N A
F K M L C R M I N I S I A R
Q T G I N G E R U T J N C H
V A N I L L A A U R L G K O
B G T H H K L N T C F B X A
```

Solution on Page 347

Puzzles • 163

ALGORITHMS

BASIC

COBOL

CODE

COMMANDS

COMPILER

COMPUTERS

DATA

DEBUG

DESIGN

ENGINEER

EXECUTE

EXPRESSION

FORTRAN

FUNCTIONAL

HTML

INPUT

JAVASCRIPT

LINES

LOGIC

MACHINE

MICROSOFT

NUMBER

OBJECT

PASCAL

PERL

PROGRAMS

PYTHON

RUBY

SCIENCE

SEMANTICS

SOFTWARE

SQL

SYMBOLS

SYNTAX

TECHNOLOGY

TYPE

Programming Languages

```
O T L N G I S E D O C T T C
B Y P R E E N I G N E F S N
J P A V E I N F C C O B O L
E E S U H P O O H S A H F Y
C H C C U R M N O S T C T H
T T A T T M O R M Y A O W C
P M L R A L C H P I D M A I
I L A N O I T C N U F P R S
R N D G M I G U B E D U E A
C S Y P R O G R A M S T T B
S A N O I S S E R P X E U R
A Q G B C O M P I L E R C U
V L L S E M A N T I C S E B
A S Y M B O L S E N I L X Y
J X A T N Y S C I E N C E I
L O G I C W D N U M B E R G
```

Solution on Page 347

BASTING BRUSH

BLENDER

BOTTLE OPENER

BREAD

COUNTER

DICER

DISH TOWEL

EGG BEATER

ELECTRIC KNIFE

FLOUR

FREEZER

GARBAGE CAN

GRATER

GRILL

HEAT

ISLAND

JUICER

MILK

MITT

MIXING BOWL

NUTCRACKER

PIE SERVER

PIZZA WHEEL

REFRIGERATOR

SINK

SPOONS

STIR

STOVE

SUGAR

TABLESPOON

THERMOMETER

VEGETABLES

WOODEN SPOON

Around the Kitchen

```
S T O V E G E T A B L E S K
D I C E R P I E S E R V E R
L A M I X I N G B O W L W R
E D E R E T N U O C E D O E
E I G R A Z T D T C T T O T
H S U R B G N I T S A B D E
W H G O E A U R L R R L E M
A T P A L G I S E U E E N O
Z O M S R C G G O O C N S M
Z W I I K B I B P L I D P R
I E L N L R A K E F U E O E
P L I K F K O G N A J R O H
H F R E E Z E R E R T L N T
E O R E T A R G R C I E S T
A E N O O P S E L B A T R I
T H R E K C A R C T U N S M
```

Solution on Page 348

BALTIMORE

BOSTON

CHARLOTTE

CHICAGO

CLEVELAND

COLUMBUS

DALLAS

FRESNO

HOUSTON

INDIANAPOLIS

KANSAS CITY

LONG BEACH

LOS ANGELES

MIAMI

MINNEAPOLIS

NEW YORK CITY

OAKLAND

OKLAHOMA CITY

PHILADELPHIA

RALEIGH

SACRAMENTO

SAN ANTONIO

SAN FRANCISCO

SAN JOSE

ST. LOUIS

WASHINGTON

```
D N A L E V E L C O A E K B
E R O M I T L A B O S T O N
S A I H P L E D A L I H P K
O I A S A C R A M E N T O A
J O W Z K I M A I M Y D I F
N I A O A K L A N D T W H L
A N S A N F R A N C I S C O
S O H W S P H C E O C R A S
Y T I C A M O H A L K O E A
D N N F S H U I P U R S B N
A A G R C G S C O M O T G G
L N T E I I T A L B Y L N E
L A O S T E O G I U W O O L
A S N N Y L N O S S E U L E
S I L O P A N A I D N I U S
M K C H A R L O T T E S Y V
```

Solution on Page 348

ANALYSIS	LINEAGES
ANCESTRY	LOCATION
BAPTISM	MARRIAGES
BIRTH	MOTHER
BLOODLINE	NAMES
BORN	PARENTS
BROTHER	PAST
CENSUS	PEDIGREES
CHILDREN	PEOPLE
COUSIN	RECORDS
DATA	RELATIVES
DNA	RESEARCH
FAMILIES	SIBLINGS
FATHER	SOCIETY
HERALDRY	SOFTWARE
HISTORICAL	SURNAME
KINSHIP	TRADITIONS
LIBRARY	TREE

Family Tree

```
S E G A E N I L D O O L B P
U U T P K S O F T W A R E R
P A S T N O I T A C O L T E
D D N N R O B E I M B F Y L
H C R A E S E R E A R A R A
B Y T E I C O S N R O M D T
A S N O I T I D A R T I L I
P Y R T S E C N A I H L A V
T R S I S Y L A N A E I R E
I A H F J P E D I G R E E S
S R N C H I L D R E N S H T
M B S G N I L B I S E M A N
N I S U O C P S U R N A M E
E L P O E P P S D R O C E R
K X R E H T A F B I R T H A
M O T H E R K I N S H I P P
```

Solution on Page 348

BARK

BASEBALL

BOARDS

BOTTLE

BULLETIN

BUOYANT

CAP

CHAMPAGNE

CORK OAK

CORKSCREW

ELASTICITY

FLOATS

FLOORING

HANDLES

INDUSTRY

MATERIAL

NATURAL

PORTUGAL

RECYCLING

SEAL

STOPPER

SUBERIN

TILES

TISSUE

TREE

WALL

WINE

WOOD

Cork

```
H  T  N  A  Y  O  U  B  O  A  R  D  S  R
Q  N  A  T  U  R  A  L  R  F  B  A  R  K
R  C  L  S  S  S  T  A  O  L  F  F  E  U
N  H  A  N  D  L  E  S  I  B  Z  L  P  F
O  A  E  L  O  L  A  G  U  T  R  O  P  I
F  M  S  L  L  A  W  C  D  D  D  O  O  W
K  P  K  A  O  K  R  O  C  T  N  R  T  T
V  A  B  B  E  N  O  R  X  S  E  I  S  H
E  G  U  E  U  W  A  K  L  C  L  N  U  G
U  N  L  S  S  Y  X  S  Y  A  S  G  B  V
S  E  L  A  S  T  I  C  I  T  Y  O  E  V
Q  N  E  B  I  V  L  R  S  F  T  R  R  P
U  L  T  W  T  I  E  E  E  T  N  P  I  U
M  J  I  P  N  T  E  W  L  E  Z  L  N  L
F  N  N  G  A  E  C  E  I  R  R  Z  A  R
E  S  B  M  V  C  L  L  T  T  L  T  I  R
```

Solution on Page 348

ACCUMULATION	MELT
AVALANCHE	MOGULS
BANK	PACK
BLIZZARD	PLOUGH
BLOWING	SHOVEL
CAP	SKIING
CHAINS	SLEDDING
DRIFT	SLUSH
FLAKES	SNOW BLOWER
FLURRIES	SNOWBALL FIGHT
FORT	SNOWBOARD
FREEZE	SNOWFALL
FROSTBITE	SNOWMOBILE
IGLOO	STORM
LODGE	THROWER

```
P  Z  Y  I  V  W  Z  S  T  F  I  R  D  P
S  N  O  W  F  A  L  L  E  Z  E  E  R  F
G  N  O  I  T  A  L  U  M  U  C  C  A  P
A  N  O  K  G  J  R  S  O  H  D  V  O  V
D  Y  I  W  S  C  E  H  G  A  R  G  B  F
P  D  X  W  B  N  W  U  U  J  A  D  W  L
T  C  R  W  O  A  O  H  L  O  Z  V  O  T
S  H  O  V  E  L  L  W  S  A  Z  K  N  F
T  E  U  K  P  Y  B  L  M  E  I  I  S  L
O  C  K  K  I  P  W  P  F  O  L  N  O  U
R  H  N  A  G  H  O  A  C  I  B  D  M  R
M  A  V  A  L  A  N  C  H  E  G  I  E  R
B  I  T  R  O  F  S  K  I  E  O  H  L  I
L  N  N  M  O  F  R  O  S  T  B  I  T  E
U  S  K  I  I  N  G  N  I  D  D  E  L  S
Q  L  K  Q  M  P  R  E  W  O  R  H  T  Z
```

Solution on Page 349

ALL SAINTS DAY

ASH WEDNESDAY

BASTILLE DAY

CHRISTMAS

CINCO DE MAYO

COLUMBUS DAY

EARTH DAY

FATHER'S DAY

FLAG DAY

FOURTH OF JULY

GOOD FRIDAY

GROUNDHOG DAY

GUY FAWKES DAY

KWANZAA

LABOR DAY

LUNAR NEW YEAR

MARDI GRAS

MAY DAY

NEW YEAR'S DAY

PRESIDENTS' DAY

RAMADAN

ROSH HASHANAH

VALENTINE'S DAY

On the Calendar

```
Y Y A D G O H D N U O R G Q
A P A Y A D S U B M U L O C
D P R D Y A D I R F D O O G
S B V E S A R G I D R A M J
R Y A D S E K W A F Y U G C
A L L S A I N T S D A Y K I
E U E U T L D D Y N E T W N
Y S N A J I A E E A F P A C
W A T Q R F L B N W D I N O
E M I B K T O L O T H Y Z D
N T N Z O F H H E R S S A E
R S E G O J G D T D D D A M
A I S N A D A M A R A A A A
N R D F L A G D A Y U Y Y Y
U H A N A H S A H H S O R O
L C Y A D S R E H T A F F Z
```

Solution on Page 349

PUZZLES • **177**

AMERICA	PRODUCTS
BUSINESS	PROFIT
BUYING	PURCHASING
CAPITALIST	RETAIL
CONSUMER	RIGHTS
COST	SELL
CREDIT	SERVICES
DEMAND	SHOPPING
DESIRE	SOCIETY
ECONOMY	SPEND
GOODS	STATUS
INDUSTRY	STORE
MALL	SUPPLY
MARKETING	TRADE
MONEY	WANT
PACKAGING	WASTE
PEOPLE	WEALTH

Consumerism

```
Y M J G N I S A H C R U P G
P L Z R P A C K A G I N G X
Z B P S H O P P I N G T P G
T U J P G N I Y U B D Q A O
S S Y K U T U N N Z D Q U O
G I T W A S T E D E M A N D
H N E L D N E P S U T A T S
R E I S E R V I C E S Y U E
E S C T L J R L C I M T P L
T S O S E E A T O O Z P R L
A J S X C K M O N E Y R O Y
I S T H G I R O S A W O D R
L T Z W V T C A U N W F U M
P E O P L E V A M E R I C A
H T L A E W C R E D I T T L
C O S T R A D E R O T S S L
```

Solution on Page 349

BLUE RIBBON

CARNIVAL

CAROUSEL

CONCERTS

CORN DOGS

CORN ON THE COB

COTTON CANDY

DISPLAYS

ENTERTAINMENT

EXHIBITS

FAIRGROUND

FERRIS WHEEL

GAMES

ICE CREAM

LIVESTOCK

NACHOS

PARADE

PETTING ZOO

PIE-EATING CONTEST

PIGS

POPCORN

PRIZES

RIDES

SODAS

TRADE SHOW

ZIPPER RIDE

County Fairs

```
E G A M E S C D T S A D O S
X N W Q D G A N S T E C I G
H R T P I C R U E R U L Z I
I O L E R O N O T E T S T P
B C E T R T I R N C M G R P
I P S T E T V G O N K O A R
T O U I P O A R C O C D D I
S P O N P N L I G C O N E Z
O I R G I C M A N J T R S E
H C A Z Z A S F I M S O H S
C E C O R N O N T H E C O B
A C M O E D A R A P V N W X
N R U K K Y U S E D I R T R
F E R R I S W H E E L N G S
H A R B L U E R I B B O N N
Q M I X R D I S P L A Y S X
```

Solution on Page 349

ADAMS BLVD.

ALLEYWAY

BACK STREET

BOULEVARD

CENTER AVE.

CHERRY ST.

CHURCH AVE.

ELM STREET

FOREST ROAD

LINCOLN AVE.

MAIN DRAG

MILL ST.

NORTH ST.

OAK STREET

PARK AVENUE

PINE STREET

SIDE STREET

SPRING ST.

SUNSET BLVD.

WALL STREET

WALNUT ST.

WASHINGTON

WILLOW AVE.

WILSON ROAD

Street Names

```
N  I  F  Q  G  M  T  S  G  N  I  R  P  S
O  J  B  O  U  L  E  V  A  R  D  Q  N  U
T  E  P  A  R  K  A  V  E  N  U  E  G  N
G  V  P  I  N  E  S  T  R  E  E  T  A  S
N  A  S  I  D  E  S  T  R  E  E  T  R  E
I  W  I  W  T  S  H  T  R  O  N  H  D  T
H  O  B  A  C  K  S  T  R  E  E  T  N  B
S  L  W  L  E  V  A  N  L  O  C  N  I  L
A  L  A  L  D  V  L  B  S  M  A  D  A  V
W  I  L  S  O  N  R  O  A  D  C  D  M  D
P  W  N  T  S  Y  R  R  E  H  C  S  I  O
C  H  U  R  C  H  A  V  E  A  G  M  L  N
I  V  T  E  V  A  R  E  T  N  E  C  L  B
P  Y  S  E  L  M  S  T  R  E  E  T  S  P
B  Z  T  T  E  E  R  T  S  K  A  O  T  A
E  Y  A  W  Y  E  L  L  A  A  M  U  H  I
```

Solution on Page 350

ANATOMY	GEOLOGY
ANCIENT	HUMAN
ANIMALS	JURASSIC
BIOLOGY	LAB
BIRDS	LIFE
BONES	MESOZOIC
DATING	MUSEUM
DINOSAURS	OCEAN
DISCOVERY	ORGANISMS
DNA	PALEOZOIC
EARTH	REPTILES
ECOSYSTEM	RESEARCH
EROSION	ROCKS
EVOLUTION	SCIENTIST
EXPERIMENT	SITE
EXTINCTION	STUDY
FISH	TAXONOMY
FOSSILS	TRIASSIC
FUNGI	

```
C B I O L O G Y D U T S A B
I M U S E U M S L A M I N A
O N O I S O R E S E A R C H
Z J F L T G P E N S D R I B
O U U A Q L H A P H N W E S
E R N B R T M N T T O S N S
L A G S R U A S O N I D T L
A S I A H G I T O E T L G I
P S E N N T R I C M U S E S
C I E I N I T O E I L K O S
A C T E A C S F A R O C L O
N A I S N Y I M N E V O O F
D C S I S L Y Y S P E R G I
S I T T Y M O N O X A T Y S
C X E D I S C O V E R Y T H
E M E S O Z O I C S E N O B
```

Solution on Page 350

AEROSPACE	PLAN
ANALYSIS	PROBLEMS
BRIDGES	PRODUCTION
BUILDING	PROFESSION
CHEMICAL	REGULATION
COLLEGE	RESEARCH
COMPUTERS	SAFETY
CONSTRUCT	SOFTWARE
EDUCATION	STRUCTURES
INDUSTRIAL	SYSTEMS
INGENUITY	TECHNICAL
JOB	TECHNOLOGY
KNOWLEDGE	TRAIN
MATERIALS	UNIVERSITY
MECHANICS	WORK
PHYSICS	

```
S B S L Y G O L O N H C E T
A U E A U M P R O B L E M S
F I G I S L A I R E T A M W
E L D R N S T B O J N Q A O
T D I T A A H C R A E S E R
Y I R S L C O L L E G E R K
T N B U P P H Y S I C S O T
I G G D S Y S T E M S T S K
S E S N O I T C U D O R P N
R N O I S S E F O R P U A O
E U F O L A C I M E H C C W
V I T C O N S T R U C T E L
I T W C I N O I T A C U D E
N Y A A C O M P U T E R S D
U T R C L A C I N H C E T G
I T E M E C H A N I C S O E
```

Solution on Page 350

ARMSTRONG	GOODMAN
BECHET	HINES
BENNETT	HOLIDAY
BOLDEN	JAMES
BROWN	JARREAU
BUBLÉ	MARTIN
CALLOWAY	MCSHANN
COLTRANE	MILLER
CONNICK	NICHOLS
CROSBY	PARKER
DAVIS	SINATRA
DORSEY	TORMÉ
ELLINGTON	WALLER
FITZGERALD	WEBSTER
GILLESPIE	

```
N S M X P A R K E R F J S D
T E H C E B S B C V H U E D
O S D Y S L O H C I N F M Z
R R I L Y H Y F N O N I A D
M Q E N O E A E B J C N J Z
E Y N H A B S N A M D O O G
D A A E V T U R N O U E I C
H D R E N A R B O U G L A Y
F I T Z G E R A L D L L R B
Z L L R A E Q M A E L I E S
G O O U T A I V S O N N L O
Q H C S E L I P W T N G L R
J H B D L S I A L E R T A C
P E S E B E Y N T B R O W N
W Y R X M A R T I N E N N S
P H V B M I S A Y U J X K G
```

Solution on Page 350

ACTIVITY	LEG PRESS
AEROBICS	LIFTING
ATHLETIC	MUSCLE
BICYCLE	NUTRITION
BOXING	OBESITY
CARDIO	PILATES
CIRCUIT	RUNNING
CYCLING	SPORTS
DIET	STRENGTH
ELLIPTICAL	STRETCHING
EQUIPMENT	SWIMMING
FITNESS	TRAINING
GYM	TREADMILL
HEALTHY	WALKING
HEART RATE	WEIGHT
HIKING	YOGA
JUMP ROPE	

```
H E A L T H Y D D W M S N I
U A N W R U I I G U W S U S
B P I L A T E S S I S E T C
O S Z J I T L C M T E R R I
X D S U N Z L M R T E P I B
I H T M I E I O A T Q G T O
N D R P N N P R C R U E I R
G O E R G S T H T E I L O E
E N I N O V R I I I A P O N A
I D G P A N C K V D M B L E
K R T E G I A I I M E E I L
L A H M R D L N T I N S F C
A C Y C L I N G Y L T I T Y
W G U Y P B A T H L E T I C
F I T N E S S J A G O Y N I
T H G I E W R U N N I N G B
```

Solution on Page 351

BIRTH

BOND

BROTHER

CHILDHOOD

CHILDREN

CLOSE

ETYMOLOGY

FAMILY

FATHER

FIGHTING

FOSTER

FRIEND

FULL

GENETICS

GIRL

HALF

HOME

JEALOUSY

KINSHIP

LOVE

MIDDLE

MOTHER

OLDER

PARENTS

RELATIVE

RIVALRY

SHARE

SISTER

STEP

TOGETHER

TWINS

YOUNGEST

Siblings

```
A N P A R Y S U O L A E J I
E T I N M U Z C L O S E K Q
R M O F R J G P I H S N I K
A Z O L Q C R E H T O M H E
H V U H F R I E N D E G K R
S N I W T P J V O X I N R T
T I X Y G O L O M Y T E E O
N S G I A B H L F S L R H G
E U N M I D D L E A L D T E
R G I R L X A G T B S L A T
A E T I F H N I Y O I I F H
P H H J K U V J L N S H S E
N C G T O E L D I D T C A R
O U I Y O U E L M P E T S A
N E F A U R I V A L R Y D H
U F P T G A B K F O S T E R
```

Solution on Page 351

PUZZLES • **193**

ABSTRACT	ISO SPEED
ALBUM	LANDSCAPE
ANSEL ADAMS	LARGE FORMAT
BACKLIGHT	LIGHT METER
BLUR	LIGHTING
CLOSE-UP	MACRO
COMPOSITION	MATTE
CROPPING	PHOTOSHOP
DARKROOM	PORTFOLIO
DEPTH OF FIELD	PROCESSING
DEVELOPMENT	SHUTTER
ENLARGER	SILHOUETTE
EXPOSURE	SPOOL
FILM	TELEPHOTO
GEORGE EASTMAN	TRIPOD
IMAGES	

Photography

```
M O I L O F T R O P R V N S
O G N I S S E C O R P A H T
O D O G C I C F I L M U H E
R E I H E S L M A T T E G L
K P T T N O O L S T R G N E
R T I M L S S A E N U M I P
A H S E A P E R E E L A T H
D O O T R E U G T M B C H O
E F P E G E P E T P T R G T
I F M R E D R F E O C O I O
M I O T R U Q O U L A P L S
A E C G S C T R O E R P K H
G L O O P S S M H V T I C O
E D P S M A D A L E S N A P
S X D O P I R T I D B G B T
E M U B L A N D S C A P E J
```

Solution on Page 351

PUZZLES • 195

AWL	GRAIN
BALSA	GRIT
BARK	GROOVE
BEAD	HAMMER
BENCH	HARDWOOD
BLADE	HINGE
BOARD	JIGSAW
BUILDING	JOINT
BURL	KNOT
CARVING	LUMBER
CHISEL	MITRE
CROSSCUT	MORTISE
DADO	PATTERN
DOVETAIL	RASP
DRILL	ROUTER
FACE	SCRAPER
FENCE	SOFTWOOD
FLUTE	SQUARE
FRAME	VENEER
GOUGE	VISE

Woodworking

```
M O I B L H Z V E N E E R D
E T U L F P W T F D R A O B
B R I A U E M A R F L T U X
L R W D Q D C C S G E N T H
D L G E O E O F X G S I E A
R K E G U O G O E I I O R E
E C R R D E W R W N H J E Z
B A T A G L R T I D C G M I
M R I I B N N A F T R E M S
U V M N D R I M U O O A A L
L I A T E V O D O Q S H H I
R N R T I R E V L L S C M N
A G T D T B E K A I C N H B
S A H I N G E B N F U E Y N
P E S I V Q D A D O T B B H
R E P A R C S T D H T V D F
```

Solution on Page 351

ABSORPTION

ACETATE

ACID

ALPHA PARTICLE

AMPLITUDE

ARGON

ATOMIC MASS

BETA PARTICLE

BUNSEN BURNER

CATHODE RAY

ELECTRIC FIELD

ELEMENT

ENZYME

FISSION

FLASK

FLUORINE

FREQUENCY

FUME HOOD

GASES

LAB COAT

METALLURGY

MIXTURES

OHM

REPULSIVE

RESISTANCE

RESONANCE

SOLIDS

SUPERCONDUCTOR

VOLT

```
M E U M Z P B F I S S I O N
I C E R H S U E K A D B O O
X N L L Y O N N L B O E R G
T A C A G L S I Z S O T E R
U N I B R I E R A O H A P A
R O T C U D N O C R E P U S
E S R O L S B U E P M A L C
S E A A L K U L T T U R S A
I R P T A S R F A I F T I T
S A A L T A N N T O Q I V H
T C H O E L E M E N T C E O
A I P V M F R N U O S L I D
N D L E I F C I R T C E L E
C R A T O M I C M A S S S R
E M Y Z N E D U T I L P M A
G A S E S F R E Q U E N C Y
```

Solution on Page 352

AMATEUR	HARNESS
AMBLE	HOOF
ARABIAN	JOCKEY
ARENA	JUMPING
BOLTING	MANE
BRIDLE	MARE
BUCKING	PONY
CANTER	POSTING
COAT	RACE
COLT	REINS
CROP	RIDING
ENGLISH	RODEO
EQUINE	SADDLE
FILLY	STALLION
FOAL	STIRRUPS
FURLONG	STRIDE
GAIT	TACK
GALLOP	TROT
GELDING	WESTERN
HALTER	WHINNY

Speaking of Horses

```
A Y D S M X Z W R O D E O G
E N A M K X H O Y E K C O J
E G E G R I D I N G I A G R
B R H R N W E S T E R N K R
R F A N A B A G E L X T S T
I I Y M G O M A N D R E O F
D L B P N L A S I I E R O N
L L T E O T T T U N T A K Y
E Y I D L I E A Q G L S P N
N J Q I R N U L E N A A O O
G U H R U G R L A I H D L P
L M U T F Y J I X K H D L K
I P P S L C B O O C O L A C
S I N O O A E N W U O E G A
H N H A R N E S S B F L J T
G G T A E C A R J G A I T Y
```

Solution on Page 352

ACTIVITIES

ADVERTISE

BEBO

BLOG

CHAT

CLASSMATES

COMMENTS

COMMUNITY

COMPUTER

CONNECTION

CONTACT

DATING

EMAIL

EVENTS

FACEBOOK

FRIENDSTER

INTERACT

INTERESTS

INTERNET

LIKE

LINKEDIN

MYSPACE

NETWORKING

ONLINE

PEOPLE

PICTURES

PLATFORM

PRIVACY

SHARING

TECHNOLOGY

TWITTER

WALL

WEBSITE

```
L G B C O N T A C T E K I L
L C L Y K S T S E R E T N I
A H O A D V E R T I S E I N
W A G M R E T U P M O C E K
R T D P M J G N I R A H S E
M E Y I W E B S I T E N O D
Y R T C O N N E C T I O N I
S E I T I V I T C A N L E N
P T N U I H I A S D T O T P
A S U R E W N M T A E G W R
C D M E N O T S N T R Y O I
E N M S I B E S E I A L R V
P E O P L E R A V N C I K A
Q I C K N B N L E G T A I C
C R K O O B E C A F D M N Y
Y F M R O F T A L P J E G K
```

Solution on Page 352

ABIGAIL	KATE
ALEXANDER	KELLY
ANDREW	MADISON
ANGELA	MATTHEW
AVA	MEGAN
BENJAMIN	MICHAEL
BRIAN	NATHAN
CHLOE	NICHOLAS
DANIEL	NOAH
DYLAN	OLIVIA
ELIZABETH	RYAN
EMILY	SARAH
EMMA	SYDNEY
ETHAN	TAYLOR
GRACE	TODD
JACOB	TYLER
JANE	WILLIAM
JASON	ZACHARY
JOSHUA	

Baby Names

```
C  T  Z  R  R  U  E  F  D  F  P  U  E  J
W  Y  C  O  N  O  A  H  S  B  B  M  O  C
D  L  J  H  A  Y  L  Z  A  N  M  I  N  B
V  E  A  A  L  Y  J  Y  R  A  H  C  A  Z
Y  R  C  C  S  O  M  L  A  H  I  H  H  H
L  D  O  A  S  O  E  A  H  T  K  A  T  E
I  Y  B  H  R  D  N  B  D  E  D  E  A  X
M  L  U  Y  D  G  A  I  S  I  B  L  N  G
E  A  A  O  E  C  J  G  C  A  S  H  B  Y
G  N  T  L  I  E  Q  A  Z  H  U  O  E  E
A  V  A  T  D  A  N  I  E  L  O  N  N  N
N  H  P  I  H  D  L  L  P  H  R  L  J  D
N  H  X  K  R  E  D  N  A  X  E  L  A  Y
Y  L  L  E  K  B  W  I  L  L  I  A  M  S
E  A  W  X  C  A  L  K  O  L  I  V  I  A
H  C  E  W  I  R  U  L  C  S  U  C  N  J
```

Solution on Page 352

ANIMALS

ARTIFACTS

AUTOGRAPHS

BOOKS

BOTTLES

BUTTONS

CANS

CDS

CHINA

COINS

CURRENCY

DISNEY

DOLLS

FIGURINES

FILMS

FURNITURE

GLASS

GUNS

HATS

JEWELRY

KEYS

MAGAZINES

MAPS

MODEL CARS

MUSIC

NEWSPAPERS

PLATES

POSTCARDS

POTTERY

RECORDS

ROCKS

SEASHELLS

STAMPS

TEAPOTS

THIMBLES

TOYS

TRAINS

WINE

```
Q Y D Y E S E N I R U G I F
B R O U H A T S S K O O B J
S E L T T O B C L A N I H C
D T L E N S D R A C T S O P
R T S A E H L W M F B N C A
O O S P W P M I I I I O U O
C P A O S A J N N L C T R E
E L L T P R T E A M P T R M
R A G S A G A R W S S U E A
O T Y P P O Y C A E T B N G
C E T M E T J E L I L R C A
K S O A R U C B N E N R Y Z
S N Y T S A M R S S D S Y I
N I S S N I U V F D I O L N
U O E S H F M U S I C D M E
G C X T O S E A S H E L L S
```

Solution on Page 353

BATHTUB

BRASS

COPPER

COUPLING

DRAINAGE

DRINKING

EQUIPMENT

FITTINGS

FIXTURES

FLANGES

HEATERS

KITCHEN

LEAD PIPE

LINES

METERS

PIPING

PLASTIC

PLUMBER

PUMPS

SEPTIC

SEWAGE

SHOWER

SINKS

SKILL

SYSTEMS

TOILETS

TOOLS

TRAP

TUBING

VALVES

WASTE

WATER MAIN

WRENCH

Plumbing

```
D N S E N I L R U L G L J C
T N E M P I U Q E N L E F J
U I V G Q D R A I N A G E Q
B A L C A X D P W R E N C H
I M A O F P I R F S L O O T
N R V U I P B K I T C H E N
G E R P T R S U X N G G P F
K T E L T Q T S T S K I L L
Z A B I I E E P U H C I S A
I W M N N G L M R E T Y N N
C R U G G A I U E A S A Q G
I O L Y S W O P S T R S B E
T K P T F E T N E E E K R S
P P I P E S B M D R T N A N
E C A W E T S A W S E I S E
S H O W E R T R A P M S S R
```

Solution on Page 353

ACCOMPLISHED

ADMIRABLE

BLUE RIBBON

DESIRABLE

DISTINCTIVE

DISTINGUISHED

EXCEPTIONAL

EXPERT

EXQUISITE

FINEST

FIRST-RATE

HIGH-GRADE

INCOMPARABLE

MERITORIOUS

OPTIMAL

PEACHY

PRIZEWINNING

STERLING

SUPERLATIVE

SUPREME

TRANSCENDENT

UNEXCELLED

WORLD-BEATING

WORLD-CLASS

Good Words

```
L X F H I G H G R A D E S M
E B I J F F I N E S T D S M
V L R L A N O I T P E C X E
I U S Y S O W N I H U E W R
T E T H U T O N S A N L O I
C R R C P R R I I D E B R T
N I A A R E L W U M X A L O
I B T E P D E Q I C R D R
T B E P M X B Z X R E I C I
S O N O E E E I E A L S L O
I N C O M P A R A B L E A U
D C L A M I T P O L E D S S
A S T E R L I N G E D M S R
X V T N E D N E C S N A R T
D E H S I U G N I T S I D E
B E V I T A L R E P U S V A
```

Solution on Page 353

ACTIVITY

AEROBATICS

AMATEUR

ARCHERY

ATHLETIC

BASEBALL

BASKETBALL

BOWLING

BOXING

CRICKET

CURLING

EQUIPMENT

ETHICS

FOOTBALL

GAME

GOLF

GYMNASTICS

LACROSSE

MEDICINE

NUTRITION

PHYSICAL

PLAYERS

POLITICS

RECREATION

RUGBY

RULES

RUNNING

SCORE

SOFTBALL

SWIMMING

TEAM SPORT

TENNIS

TRAINING

Sporting Chance

```
A T H L E T I C U R L I N G L I N G
S C O R E Q S O F T B A L L L
R A M A T E U R U N N I N G
E Z Y N O I T I R T U N O G
Y B G U R B N G P E M A G N
A L N Y T R O P S M A E T I
L T I T M L I Y L P E G L L
P E N E F N T L L O T N H W
H K I N E I A M A L H I T O
Y C A N V B E S B I I M Y B
S I R I E D R X T T C M R O
I R T S I R C V E I S I E X
C C A C U V E X K C C W H I
A B I L A C R O S S E S C N
L N E F O O T B A L L L R G
E S N S C I T A B O R E A T
```

Solution on Page 353

ADRIATIC SEA

CAESAR

COLUMNS

CONSTANTINE

DANTE

GENOA

HADRIAN

LIBRARIES

MACHIAVELLI

MARKETS

MICHELANGELO

MOUNT VESUVIUS

MUSSOLINI

PALATINE HILL

PIETA

ROMAN FORUM

SEVEN HILLS

SISTINE CHAPEL

SPANISH STEPS

TIBER RIVER

TURIN

TYRRHENIAN SEA

VATICAN CITY

VENICE

VERONA

VILLA BORGHESE

```
T K F Y T I C N A C I T A V
E A T N S L L I H N E V E S
S M U R O F N A M O R N S J
E I M U S S O L I N I U N T
H C S N M U L O C T I S A I
G H T T I Z G E N V P E I L
R E E P I E T A U E T I N L
O L K Q N N T S T N U R E E
B A R O A S E S D I R A H V
A N A D N V H C T C I R R A
L G M O T S Q O H E N B R I
L E C N I R A S E A C I Y H
I L U N A I R D A H P L T C
V O A D R I A T I C S E A A
M P A L A T I N E H I L L M
S T I B E R R I V E R O N A
```

Solution on Page 354

ACCRA	ISLAMABAD
ADDIS ABABA	JAKARTA
ANKARA	KATHMANDU
ASUNCION	KHARTOUM
BAGHDAD	LIBREVILLE
BELMOPAN	LUANDA
BUDAPEST	MAPUTO
BUJUMBURA	MOGADISHU
CAPE TOWN	NICOSIA
COLOMBO	PHNOM PENH
COPENHAGEN	PORT LOUIS
DHAKA	QUITO
FREETOWN	RABAT
GABORONE	ULAANBAATAR
GIBRALTAR	VIENTIANE
HAVANA	

World Capitals

```
A K A H D F R E E T O W N A
C A P E T O W N I C O S I A
H B B H E L L I V E R B I L
N E G A H N E P O C A V N T
E L D I B S I U O L T R O P
P M J A K A R T A W A A I M
M O G A D I S H U T A T C U
O P I V G H P I S S B L N O
N A C S I Q G E D U N A U T
H N O O L E P A J D A R S R
P A L T T A N U B N A B A A
A V O I D U M T K C L I D H
C A M U D B P A I O U G N K
C H B Q U M R A B A T B A F
R T O R K A T H M A N D U U
A G A B O R O N E G D E L G
```

Solution on Page 354

AIRPLANE

ATTRACTIONS

CANCUN

CASH

CREDIT CARDS

CUSTOMS

DRIVE

ENTERTAINMENT

FAST FOOD

FREEWAY

HIKING

HOT TUB

INN

MAP

MINIVAN

RESERVATIONS

REST STOPS

RIVER RAFTING

ROAD SIGNS

SCENIC ROUTE

SIGHTSEEING

SKYDIVING

SNACKS

SPA

SUITCASE

THEME PARKS

TOURIST TRAPS

TRANSPORTATION

TRAVEL GAMES

Take a Trip

```
J T B T S K Y D I V I N G S
S C E N I C R O U T E E D N
I T H E M E P A R K S R S A
G S I M R H P L Y A I D P C
H N K N I W O A C V H R A K
T G I I N N W T E J S E R S
S I N A N E I R T P A S T D
E S G T E U R V O U C E T R
E D R R S A M T A Q B R S A
I A F E F C S A A N J V I C
N O I T A T R O P S N A R T
G R I N S M O T S U C T U I
M N C E N A L P R I A I O D
G U R F A S T F O O D O T E
N P A T T R A C T I O N S R
M T R A V E L G A M E S X C
```

Solution on Page 354

AFRICAN

ALLIGATORS

ASIAN

BATS

BOBCAT

CAGES

CARIBOU

CHIMPANZEE

COUGAR

CROCODILES

ELEPHANTS

FAUNA

FLAMINGOES

FROGS

GORILLA

HIPPOPOTAMUS

KOOKABURRA

KUDU

MOOSE

MOUNTAIN GOATS

NORTH AMERICAN

ORANGUTANS

PETTING ZOOS

PRIMATES

REPTILES

RHINOCEROS

SKUNKS

SNOW CONES

SOUTH AMERICAN

```
M S R O T A G I L L A N E S
N O R T H A M E R I C A N K
S U U U N A I S A Z M C A U
T T S N D N O O G H O I R N
N H G T T U G O U I O R R K
A A O A S A K Z O P S F U S
H M R L N F I G C P E A B N
P E F L A M I N G O E S A O
E R T I T S X I G P Z E K W
L I A R U Q E T S O N L O C
E C C O G L G T T T A I O O
O A B G N C E E A A P T K N
M N O L A M A P B M M P S E
U O B I R A C G F U I E R S
C R O C O D I L E S H R B J
R H I N O C E R O S C L P S
```

Solution on Page 354

BRAN

CHEERIOS

CLUSTERS

CORN POPS

CORNFLAKES

CRISPIX

CRUNCHY

FIBER ONE

FRUITY

GRANOLA

HONEY NUT

HONEYCOMB

KASHI

KELLOGG'S

KIX

LIFE

MUESLI

OATMEAL

PEBBLES

POST

RICE CHEX

SPECIAL K

SUGAR POPS

TOTAL

TRIX

WHEAT CHEX

WHEATIES

Breakfast Cereals

```
Y T G E H W J S B X P Z M G
T U N I O A T M E A L F D I
I X A K G S O I R E E H C E
U C R U N C H Y K I X E F M
R W B L Y P C N X E C I G C
F I B E R O N E H X L R R S
V D N S Q X H C I T U I E L
N O I U M C E R U S S I S A
H K L G T C T N E P T P P T
I A S A I S Y L I A E U O O
E S E R O E B X E C R M P T
O H U P N B K H I V S K N I
W I M O E J W A L O N A R G
Q M H P K E L L O G G S O P
Z E X S E K A L F N R O C X
P N B C G U K W R Q U P S I
```

Solution on Page 355

AUTISM

AUTONOMY

BABY

BEHAVIOR

BIRTH

BRAIN

CHANGES

CHILDHOOD

CHILDREN

COGNITIVE

EDUCATION

EMOTIONAL

GENETICS

GROWTH

INFANT

LANGUAGE

LEARNING

LOVE

MENTAL

NEWBORN

NURTURE

NUTRITION

PARENTS

PHYSICAL

PLAYING

PRESCHOOL

PSYCHOLOGY

PUBERTY

SKILLS

STUDY

TEACHING

TEETHING

THEORIES

TODDLER

Child Development

```
G H H T R I B C H A N G E S
E L N B P R E S C H O O L T
N E R D L I H C P N I E E U
E A O L A T A T H U T V M D
T R B A Y P V N Y R I N O Y
I N W T I S I A S T R I T T
C I E N N Y O F I U T A I R
S N N E G C R N C R U R O E
P G S M J H G I A E N B N B
A N K D O O H D L I H C A U
R I I Y C L M S I T U A L P
E H L B N O I T A C U D E S
N C L A N G U A G E V O L K
T A S B C Y M O N O T U A D
S E I R O E H T O D D L E R
N T E E T H I N G R O W T H
```

Solution on Page 355

ANDES	MONTSERRAT
ASPENS	MOUNT EVEREST
ATLAS	MOUNT MCKINLEY
CAMPING	OLYMPUS
CHAIN	RAINIER
EIGER	RECREATION
ELEVATION	SINAI
FAULT	SKIING
FOREST	SLOPE
HIKE	SNOWDONIA
ICE	SUGARLOAF
KILIMANJARO	VOLCANO
LAKES	WASATCH
LONGS PEAK	WEISSHORN
LUMBER	WETTERHORN
MAROON BELLS	WHITNEY
MINING	
MONT BLANC	

Mountain View

```
R  I  G  W  E  I  S  S  H  O  R  N  W  A
Y  A  N  D  E  S  H  R  F  T  O  W  W  S
E  N  I  A  H  C  E  A  A  I  E  M  Y  P
N  I  I  N  T  G  O  R  T  T  O  E  Z  E
T  S  K  A  I  L  R  A  T  N  L  R  L  N
I  T  S  E  R  E  V  E  T  N  U  O  M  S
H  A  K  A  S  E  R  B  I  M  N  A  R  F
W  I  G  T  L  H  L  K  I  G  R  E  A  A
H  U  N  E  O  A  C  N  S  O  C  L  I  U
S  O  L  R  N  M  I  P  O  R  G  U  N  L
M  E  N  C  T  N  E  N  E  N  A  M  O  T
G  S  K  N  G  A  B  A  I  T  Q  B  D  S
C  L  U  A  K  E  T  P  L  I  C  E  W  E
L  O  K  I  L  I  M  A  N  J  A  R  O  R
M  P  R  L  O  A  S  V  O  L  C  A  N  O
K  E  S  N  C  A  O  L  Y  M  P  U  S  F
```

Solution on Page 355

ANATOMY	LABORATORY
ANIMALS	LIFE
BACTERIA	MEDICINE
BOTANY	MICROSCOPE
CELLULAR	MOLECULES
CHEMISTRY	NUCLEUS
CLASS	ORGANISMS
DARWIN	PHYSIOLOGY
DNA	PROTEIN
ECOLOGY	RESEARCH
EVOLUTION	SCIENCE
FUNCTION	SPECIES
GENETICS	STRUCTURE
GROWTH	STUDY
HEREDITY	TAXONOMY
HUMAN	TISSUES
KINGDOM	

Biology

```
C E L L U L A R D A R W I N
A N D A H G N I E T O R P A
Z I S Z B N O I T C N U F M
S C E Y G O L O I S Y H P U
P I U T I I R E S E A R C H
E D S I E T B A N I M A L S
C E S D E U A N T L I F E A
I M I E R L C A S O C L C O
E O T R U O T T U H R P N R
S D A E T V E O E Y O Y E G
Y G X H C E R M L G S D I A
N N O T U U I Y C O C U C N
A I N W R S A L U L O T S I
T K O O T N A N N O P S M S
O G M R S S E L U C E L O M
B F Y G S K G E N E T I C S
```

Solution on Page 355

ALMONDS	LETTUCE
AVOCADO	MUSHROOMS
BACON BITS	OLIVES
BALSAMIC	PICKLES
BLUE CHEESE	RANCH
BROCCOLI	RED ONION
CAESAR	SPINACH
CARROTS	SPROUTS
CAULIFLOWER	SQUASH
CHICKEN	THOUSAND ISLAND
CROUTONS	TOMATO
CUCUMBER	TUNA
EGGS	VINAIGRETTE
GARLIC	
HONEY MUSTARD	
ITALIAN	

Salad Toppings

```
C A E S A R O H L N B M W B
A R S P I N A C H R U M V P
R P E A L M O N D S B A I D
R D L B V G O A H L V C N H
O R K Y M N A R U O I A A S
T A C K A U O E C G L U I A
S T I B N O C A B S O L G U
T S P G M H D U I M C I R Q
U U D S E O T D C R C F E S
O M R E D O N I O N O L T E
R Y S P M A M U H M R O T V
P E T A S A T O Q B B W E I
S N T U S O E C U T T E L L
B O O L N E K C I H C R O O
L H A S N A I L A T I F P V
T B E G G S G A R L I C I D
```

Solution on Page 356

AUNT POLLY

BECKY

BIBLE

BLOOD OATH

CAVE

COURTROOM

DR. ROBINSON

ENGAGEMENT

FENCE

GOLD

GRAVEYARD

HUCKLEBERRY FINN

INJUN JOE

ISLAND

JOE HARPER

MARK TWAIN

MISSISSIPPI RIVER

MISSOURI

MURDER

POTTER

SCHOOL

SID

ST. PETERSBURG

TOM SAWYER

TREASURE

WARTS

WIDOW DOUGLAS

The Adventures of Tom Sawyer

```
M G O L D R R O B I N S O N N
I H H W L O J V X Q O H D N N
S T P E T E R S B U R G L I
S A L G U O D W O D I W G F
I O U I S S M U R D E R R Y
S D S N M I S S O U R I A R
S O C J T V D N A L S I V R
I O H U M P C D K W U O E E
P L O N A X O E B X Y P Y B
P B O J R P U L V I R E A E
I E L O K V R I L A B C R L
R C E E T P T X H Y C L D K
I K C W W T R E A S U R E C
V Y N Y A P O T T E R G L U
E Y E U I J O W A R T S B H
R V F T N E M E G A G N E N
```

Solution on Page 356

BASE HIT

BASE LINE

BAT

BATTERS BOX

BENCH

BULLPEN

BUNT

CATCHER

DOUBLE PLAY

DUGOUT

FIELD

FOUL BALL

FULL COUNT

GLOVE

GRAND SLAM

HELMET

HITTER

HOME RUN

INNINGS

LINE DRIVE

MOUND

OUTFIELD

PINCH HITTER

PITCHER

SAFE

SCOREBOARD

STRIKE ZONE

TAG OUT

UMPIRE

WALK

WORLD SERIES

```
T N U B U L L P E N Z B M U
A T S F A W O N U R E M O H
G R P T D S C C F N P U K Z
O E A C R J E O C R T R U P
U H D X A I U H F F E V M T
T C H U O L K S I T K Y P S
U T X O B S R E T T A B I G
O I N A E T L I Z L L B R N
G P L U R D H R P O I A E I
U L N S O H D E Y S N S H N
D N B W C C L S Z D E E C N
G M A N S B L D S R D L T I
R L I M U V E L E N R I A W
K P O O I Q A R U E I N C K
L P D V G M U O J F V E Q U
T E M L E H M W G H E F A S
```

Solution on Page 356

AGENTS

APARTMENTS

APPRAISAL

BANK

BROKER

BUILDING

BUSINESS

BUYING

CLOSING

COMMERCIAL

COMMON LAW

CONTRACT

DUPLEX

EQUITY

FOR SALE

HOMES

HOUSING

INTEREST

INVESTMENT

LAND

LEASE

LICENSE

LISTING

LOANS

LOCATION

MARKET

MORTGAGES

OFFER

OWNERS

PRICE

PROPERTY

REALTOR

RENT

SALES

SELLING

TAXES

VALUE

VIEW

YARD

```
R E E S N E C I L B V G H L
P Q E Z L O C A T I O N A I
B U S I N E S S E B V I G S
P I A A W I R W K U A S E T
O T E P A S E C R I L U N I
S Y L R L E N O A L U O T N
T T P O N X W M M D E H S G
C P N P O A O M K I C N E N
A T N E M T S E V N I Y R I
R I K R M M O R T G A G E S
T O T T O T E C I R P B T O
N N T Y C J R I D H E S N L
O B E L S E L A S R O F I C
C C A R A X E L P U D M F G
G N I L L E S S N A O L E O
D B R O K E R G N I Y U B S
```

Solution on Page 356

ACADIA PARK

BOSTON

BURLINGTON

CAPE COD

CONNECTICUT

HARTFORD

MAINE

MANCHESTER

MARTHA'S VINEYARD

MASSACHUSETTS

NANTUCKET

NEW HAMPSHIRE

NEW HAVEN

PATRIOTS

PLYMOUTH

PORTLAND

PROVIDENCE

RHODE ISLAND

SALEM

VERMONT

WHITE MOUNTAINS

WORCESTER

```
A N Z K R A P A I D A C A J
K E C N E D I V O R P A I D
D W X D R O F T R A H P R N
R H L N I R B H T Y W E H A
E A Y A H O U N U E B C O L
T V Y N S H R G C N S O D T
S E C T P F L P I I T D E R
E N O U M S I L T V O A I O
C N Z C A A N Y C S I J S P
R X N K H L G M E A R S L O
O J X E W E T O N H T O A O
W H I T E M O U N T A I N S
W T O E N X N T O R P C D J
K S T T E S U H C A S S A M
R E T S E H C N A M A I N E
P T N O M R E V J O F U Z Q
```

Solution on Page 357

ALCOHOL

BELLAGIO FOUNTAIN

BRIDGES

BULLETINS

CASINOS

CROSSWALK

EIFFEL TOWER

HOTELS

LAS VEGAS BLVD.

LASER LIGHTS

MARQUEES

MONORAIL

NEON LIGHTS

PALM TREES

PEDESTRIAN

PIRATE SHOW

RESTAURANTS

ROLLER COASTER

STATUE OF LIBERTY

STATUES

TAXICABS

VOLCANO

The Las Vegas Strip

```
G L V Y L S Y N S C N M O Z
D N P T O T N T E K I A N F
V V E R L N E K U R A R A K
N L L E L A O B T T T Q C E
A I F B A R N R A A N U L I
I A E I S U L I T X U E O F
R R F L E A I D S I O E V F
T O P F R T G G N C F S K E
S N A O L S H E Z A O N L L
E O L E I E T S V B I I A T
D M M U G R S V W S G T W O
E C T T H O T E L S A E S W
P I R A T E S H O W L L S E
U R E T S A O C R E L L O R
B M E S O N I S A C E U R Q
J V S L O H O C L A B B C N
```

Solution on Page 357

ALBANY	HELENA
ATLANTA	HONOLULU
AUGUSTA	JACKSON
AUSTIN	JUNEAU
BISMARCK	LANSING
BOISE	LINCOLN
BOSTON	MADISON
CARSON CITY	NASHVILLE
CHEYENNE	OLYMPIA
COLUMBIA	PHOENIX
COLUMBUS	RALEIGH
CONCORD	SACRAMENTO
DENVER	SANTA FE
DES MOINES	ST. PAUL
DOVER	TOPEKA
HARTFORD	TRENTON

State Capitals

```
Y Q P H O E N I X R E V O D
J V E Q A T N A L T A M L A
U M F K L H O N O L U L U V
N H A Y A J A K E P O T A F
E E T R N M U C C Y F P P C
A L N A S A C R A M E N T O
U E A L I D C A R D X H S L
N N S E N I O M S E D A C U
O A H I G S L S O N R R I M
T Y V G K O U I N V O T A B
S N I H Z N M B C E C F I I
O A L X E X B N I R N O P A
B B L A U G U S T A O R M G
D L E B O I S E Y G C D Y N
J A C K S O N L O C N I L K
N I T S U A Q T R E N T O N
```

Solution on Page 357

BABYSITTER

BEST FRIENDS

CANDLES

CHAMPAGNE

CHINA

CRYSTAL

DIAMOND

DINNER

EMERALD

FLOWERS

GIFTS

GOLD

HUSBAND

JEWELRY

LACE

LOVE

MARRIAGE

MOVIE

PARTNERS

PEARLS

PLATINUM

ROSES

RUBY

SAPPHIRE

SILVER

WEDDING

WIFE

WINE

Wedding Anniversary

```
A T Y Y Q K S D T W F B G E
J A S B L C H A M P A G N E E
Z D D D U S A S K B B I I H
Y E D P N R S N Y C W F D U
E F L O W E R S D Y D T D U N
O H N M U N I T A L P S E M
E T V A K T M R O S E S W C
M K S I T R Y G F M H S R K
F A D E C A L V F T U Y G X
R E R I H P P A S C S J X W
E M E R A L D L T T B E K U
V A N I I M R C A T A W B W
L L N W V A O L U Z N E O Z
I R I I E O G N O D D L N R
S F D P H W M E D V C R O C
E T K Q M C R P Z F E Y A L
```

Solution on Page 357

PUZZLES • 245

AFTER	MUCH
ARE	MUST
BEEN	NOW
BEFORE	NUMBER
COULD	OTHER
DID	PART
DOWN	SHE
EACH	SOME
FIND	SUCH
GET	THAT
HAVE	THEY
HOW	THIS
ITS	TIME
LIKE	TWO
LONG	USE
LOOK	WERE
MADE	WHAT
MAKE	WILL
MORE	WOULD
MOST	YEARS

```
I  F  V  G  G  C  D  N  G  C  E  M  O  S
Y  O  C  Y  O  W  O  U  L  D  K  E  W  Q
B  R  G  W  O  H  W  M  M  I  I  D  O  E
I  J  T  T  S  A  N  B  M  D  L  O  N  G
R  E  D  X  S  T  M  E  A  U  M  O  S  T
P  D  T  H  E  Y  E  R  O  F  E  B  O  A
U  G  E  M  K  E  E  C  I  T  T  V  R  K
M  E  I  P  A  R  T  N  O  N  H  E  A  O
X  T  S  U  M  A  D  E  Z  H  N  E  R  H
M  L  T  O  U  T  S  E  N  Y  E  A  R  S
Z  W  R  A  C  W  X  I  F  I  E  C  E  V
Y  E  I  T  H  I  S  G  M  P  B  H  I  K
U  R  V  L  S  T  T  X  U  X  C  X  Y  E
U  E  Q  O  L  G  Z  S  Q  U  Y  G  X  A
A  T  E  S  D  T  E  D  S  Z  L  N  I  T
Z  C  B  Z  B  A  G  K  O  W  L  Z  U  D
```

Solution on Page 358

ALPHABET

ANCIENT

BIBLE

CATHOLIC

CHURCH

CLASSICAL

CLERGY

CULTURE

DEAD

FORMAL

FRENCH

GRAMMAR

GREEK

HISTORICAL

INFLECTED

ITALY

LANGUAGE

LATIUM

LEGAL

LITERATURE

MASS

MEDICINE

MEDIEVAL

MUSIC

PIG

ROMANCE

ROOTS

SCHOOLS

SCIENTIFIC

SPANISH

SPOKEN

VATICAN

VOCABULARY

WRITTEN

```
F R E N C H V A T I C A N Z
S X L K Q E R U T L U C E N
C V O C A B U L A R Y H K E
B H E M I M U S I C G H O T
T I U R U F S X Y I R I P T
E E B R U I I J P N E S S I
C R B L C T T T P F L T C R
N I E A E H A A N L C O H W
A R L F H N G R L E G R O L
M I A O S P I T E C I I O E
O R N M H P L C N T D C L G
R O G M M T A A I E I A S A
V O U M E A A N M D I L E L
I T A L Y C R C I R E C D D
Y S G R E E K G Y S O M N O
S M E D I E V A L E H F F A
```

Solution on Page 358

ALCOHOL

AROMA

BOTTLE

CABERNET

CHABLIS

CHAMPAGNE

CHARDONNAY

CHIANTI

COLOR

CORK

GRAPES

LABEL

LAMBRUSCO

MERLOT

PINOT NOIR

RED

RIESLING

ROSÉ

SAUVIGNON BLANC

SAVOUR

SÉMILLON

SHERRY

SHIRAZ

SMELL

STEMWARE

SWIRL

TASTE

VINEYARD

WHITE

WINE GLASS

WINERY

Wine Tasting

```
W H I T E L E B A L G S Z L
B C E T S A T D Z K N A X R
L O H O C L A F G E I V Q I
I T N A I H C R C O L O R W
W S T E M W A R E D S U K S
W O V M L P P R Z I E R H K
R V I N E Y A R D D I I W N
M B O S Y M S G K O R I O K
Y E A T O M E Z N A N L Q S
G Y R R E H S T Z E L N H W
C N A L B N O N G I V U A S
B V L L O N R L M I B P S Y
L S C O I T A E Y R E N I W
M U W P S S T B O T T L E
K R O C S U R B M A L L G V
J E A W S I L B A H C B A E
```

Solution on Page 358

PUZZLES • 251

ADULTHOOD

ANNOUNCEMENTS

BACCALAUREATE

CAP

CEREMONY

CLASS RING

COLLEGE

COMMENCEMENT

DIPLOMA

EDUCATION

GIFTS

GOWN

HIGH SCHOOL

HONORS

JUNE

PRINCIPAL

SCHOLARSHIP

SENIORS

STUDENTS

SUMMER

TASSEL

TEACHERS

VALEDICTORIAN

YEARBOOK

```
Y E A R B O O K N T J E H I
G K T N E M E C N E M M O C
C N D A O G T H L A I Y N A
K W I I V I A T D C N R O P
L O P R D F E A N H O E R F
L G L O S T R S O E Q M S Y
O D O T Y S U S I R L M C V
O O M C Y T A E T S H U H M
H O A I N U L L A M M S O S
C H E D O D A C C B R E L R
S T N E M E C N U O N N A P
H L U L E N C C D E C I R R
G U J A R T A S E T Q O S Y
I D F V E S B S G W Z R H Y
H A L S C O L L E G E S I N
D X H C L A P I C N I R P I
```

Solution on Page 358

ALARM

ANALOG

BAND

BATTERY

BRACELET

CASIO

CHAIN

CITIZEN

CLOCK

DATE

DIAMOND

DIGITAL

ELECTRONIC

EXPENSIVE

FASHION

GOLD

HOUR HAND

JEWELS

MECHANICAL

METAL

MINUTES

NUMBERS

PLASTIC

POCKET

QUARTZ

REPAIR

SECONDS

SEIKO

SILVER

SPRING

STOPWATCH

STRAP

SWATCH

SWISS

TIMEPIECE

WATERPROOF

WRISTWATCH

```
S O E X P E N S I V E L Z D
W K C F G O L A N A L M T Y
I I E O O C I T I Z E N R J
S E I O I S A C P C C E A E
S S P R I N G O H H T M U W
W K E P L G C A A T R G Q E
A C M R K K N I A A O T H L
T O I E E I N B L L N E O S
C L T T C E T A D D I L U R
H C T A W P O T S I C E R I
S I L W R I S T W A T C H A
I T A S E T U N I M A A A P
L S T D F A S H I O N R N E
V A E S R E B M U N W B D R
E L M L A T I G I D N A B Q
R P A R T S D N O C E S U B
```

Solution on Page 359

ACCESS

CARE

CLINICS

COVERAGE

DENTISTRY

DIAGNOSIS

DISEASE

DRUGS

EXAM

FAMILY

HEALTH

HMO

HOME

HOSPITALS

ILLNESS

INDUSTRY

INSURANCE

LAB

MEDICINE

NURSING

OFFICE

PATIENT

PHARMACY

PHYSICIAN

POLITICAL

PRIVATE

PROCEDURES

PROVIDER

RESEARCH

RIGHTS

SERVICES

SPENDING

THERAPY

TREATMENT

UNIVERSAL

VACCINES

WHO

```
N S P R I V A T E C I F F O
U C H Q T N E I T A P H W D
R L A S R E V I N U D O H R
S I R R E D I V O R P M O U
I N M E A S E C I V R E S G
N I A S T H O S P I T A L S
G C C E M V L D I S E A S E
N S Y A E C N A R U S N I R
I T M R N M B Y B I A Z M U
D H A C T Y R T S I T N E D
N G X H L T H O C T W R D E
E I E I S E N I C C A V I C
P R M U R G S S E C C A C O
S A D A A Y S S E N L L I R
F N P I H T L A E H M O N P
I Y D P O L I T I C A L E W
```

Solution on Page 359

ANIMAL	PETS
BACON	PIGLETS
BIG	PORK
BREEDING	RUNT
DOMESTIC	SAUSAGES
FARMING	SMART
FEEDING	SMELL
FERAL	SOW
FOOD	STY
HAM	SUBSPECIES
HOGS	SWINE
HOUSE PET	TAIL
LITTER	TRAINED
LIVESTOCK	TRUFFLES
MEAT	WILD BOAR
MINIATURE	

```
T B Z B S A U S A G E S T Y
T T N U R X J L Z N F E G K
S A V T P T T M I I I L D L
D E N I A R T C C D L F L S
R M I N I A T U R E K F R R
E A P C N R H N M E Q U K O
T H L I E O O S K R R R O H
T X M P G P U F R B A T S M
I A S D S L S G O H O F X G
L C T M O T E B P O B E Q N
U H E V A M P T U E D R S I
Z E P I S R E T S S L A D D
Y R L K C O T S E V I L Z E
B V Q N U L W D T S W I N E
F N A P N B I G N I M R A F
M S M X Y U B L B A C O N H
```

Solution on Page 359

BAR

BEANBAG

BEDROOM

BENCHES

BOOKCASE

CABINET

COFFEE TABLE

COUCH

CREDENZA

CUPBOARDS

DAVENPORT

DRAWERS

DRAWING BOARD

DRESSERS

END TABLE

FOOTSTOOL

HEADBOARD

HOPE CHEST

HUTCH

LIVING ROOM

LOVE SEAT

METAL

NIGHTSTAND

OTTOMAN

PLASTIC

RECLINER

SEATING

SIDEBOARD

SOFA

TABLES

WARDROBE

WICKER

WOODEN

Furniture Types

```
B T N W Y F O M F L A T E M
E E A S D R A O B P U C G O
N N M Q A W O O D E N D T O
C I O B H T O R S A R A P R
H B T U S K A G Z A E L E D
E A T T C O S N W S A K T E
S C O A B R E I E S C R S B
H O S D E D N V T I S E E O
L E A W E G O I W B E N H R
F E A R B L C L Z E L I C D
H R C O F F E E T A B L E R
D N A T S T H G I N A C P A
T R O P N E V A D B T E O W
D R E S S E R S K A D R H W
A F O S E A T I N G N J E N
C O U C H D R A O B E D I S
```

Solution on Page 359

APPRENTICE	LINES
BAIT	MANOLIN
BASEBALL	MARKET
BATTLE	MARLIN
BROTHER	OAR
FISHERMAN	OCEAN
FISHING GEAR	OLD MAN
GULF	SAILING
HARPOON	SANTIAGO
HEMINGWAY	SHACK
JOE DIMAGGIO	SHARKS
JOURNEY	SHORE
KNIFE	SKIFF

```
N E U N R U P T G F F I K S
O J N C B U S E N I L R A M
Z L S S H A R K S S R N L B
V P P J Z W C R E H T O R B
C A W R O A R A K I O T L A
O F I S H E R M A N D R P Q
J C B S X U D G C G I P E Y
F J E X X E O I N G R F A V
V W Y A W G N I M E H X E Y
Z I Q B N I L O N A M Z N E
H S C B A I T T O R G A X N
E F M M A T I R V P M G I R
J F F S I C T F U D R L I U
V B A S E B A L L X K A A O
P Y A M S U V O E U G I H J
Z Q N M Y Y X S N A G P P I
```

Solution on Page 360

APPETIZER

BACON BITS

BOWL

CAESAR

CARROTS

CHEESE

CHICKEN

COBB

CROUTONS

CUCUMBERS

DRESSING

EGGS

FRESH

FRUIT

GREENS

HAM

HEALTHY

ITALIAN

LETTUCE

MEAT

NUTS

OLIVES

ONIONS

PASTA

PEPPERS

PLATE

POTATO

RADISH

RANCH

ROMAINE

SAUCE

SEAFOOD

SIDE DISH

SPINACH

TOMATOES

TOSSED

TUNA

VEGETABLES

VINEGAR

```
E C U A S W D H J P S Y A S
R I H O N I O N S O H T S P
G R E E N S O N U T S N G E
V A T G E K F B L A O P C P
I D A G H S A A P T T U A P
N I L S S G E C U O C P S E
E S P R I H S O J U P E E R
G H T A D Z R N M E L D O S
A E I S E C C B T B R L T N
R C U E D H E I A E I O A C
O U R A I R Z T S V R I M O
M T F C S E E S E R L W O B
A T K R R G I S A A N U T B
I E Y M E N K C T O S S E D
N L K V G S P I N A C H A M
E U R A N C H M E A T U N C
```

Solution on Page 360

AIM	KITS
ALTITUDE	LAUNCHER
APOGEE	MODEL
ASSEMBLY	MOTORS
BUILD	NOSE CONE
CONSTRUCT	PAPER
DEPLOYMENT	PARACHUTE
EJECTION	PLASTIC
ENGINES	RECOVERY
ESTES	ROCKETRY
EXPLOSIVE	SAFETY
FINS	SCALE
FIRE	SHOOT
FLIGHT	SKY
FLYING	SMALL
FUN	SPACE
GLIDE	SPEED
HIGH POWER	STREAMER
HOBBY	THRUST
IGNITION	WOOD

```
S P A C E R E H C N U A L P
N N P I N Y J S E T S E M J
F R O T K V E N S R O T O M
L E G S R E C O V E R Y D I
I D E A E T T I Y M O T E A
G U E L V C I T L A C E L Q
H T E P I U O I B E K F F I
T I N H S R N N M R E A I G
H T G S O T V G E T T S N F
R L I H L S S I S S R I S U
U A N O P N A C S D Y G T N
S S E O X O S M A L L L I H
T P S T E C W E F L I I K O
D E P L O Y M E N T E D U B
C E E T U H C A R A P E G B
P D O O W U F I R E P A P Y
```

Solution on Page 360

ACTIVIST	NUN
ACTRESS	OSCAR
AWARDS	PRODUCER
BLACK	SINGER
BROADWAY	SISTER ACT
CELEBRITY	SOAPDISH
COMEDIENNE	SONGWRITER
EMMY AWARD	STAND-UP
FEMALE	STAR TREK
FILM	SUCCESSFUL
GHOST	TALENTED
GRAMMY	TELEVISION
GUINAN	THE VIEW
LION KING	TONY
MOTHER	VOICE
MOVIES	

```
T A L E N T E D S I N G E R
D B S M S O N G W R I T E R C
C R T N O S N B Y M M A R G
T O A C N V E T H E V I E W
D S K W A F I L M L S S L B
P N I I A R D E V I U L L G
D U I V B Y E U S O C A V H
D N D E I T M T W N C N K O
R I L N Y T O M S K E F E S
A E A M A V C N E I S E R T
C M W I W T W A Y N S M T V
S O A P D I S H G G F A R O
O T R N A N I U G A U L A I
G H D N O I S I V E L E T C
S E S J R E C U D O R P S E
O R I Q B S A C T R E S S N
```

Solution on Page 360

ARCHES

BIG BEND

BRYCE CANYON

CANAVERAL

CAPE COD

CAPITOL REEF

COLONIAL

DEATH VALLEY

DEVILS TOWER

DRY TORTUGAS

FIRE ISLAND

GLEN CANYON

HARPERS FERRY

JOSHUA TREE

KATMAI

KENAI FJORDS

KOBUK VALLEY

LAKE CLARK

MOUNT RAINIER

NORTH CASCADES

PADRE ISLAND

REDWOOD

ROCKY MOUNTAIN

```
K O B U K V A L L E Y M R L
S E D A C S A C H T R O N F
F E E R L O T I P A C U O I
P L F E B P C I I K A N Y K
A R I D I X O A Y A N T N E
D E R W G P L M R R A R A N
R W E O B O O T R C V A C A
E O I O E U N A E H E I N I
I T S D N S I K F E R N E F
S S L T D H A B S S A I L J
L L A K E C L A R K L E G O
A I N O Y N A C E C Y R B R
N V D J D O C E P A C Z Y D
D E I D R Y T O R T U G A S
X D D E A T H V A L L E Y J
W D E E R T A U H S O J S F
```

Solution on Page 361

ALBACORE	MARINE
BIGEYE	MELT
BIOLOGY	MERCURY
BLUEFIN	NETS
BOATS	OCEAN
CANNED	PINK
CASSEROLE	PROTEIN
CATCH	RAW
DIET	RESTAURANT
DOLPHINS	SALMON
EAT	SALT WATER
FILLET	SANDWICHES
FISHERIES	SEAFOOD
FISHING	STARKIST
FRESH	SUSHI
HELPER	SWIM
IN OIL	TIN
IN WATER	TUNA STEAK
LARGE	YELLOWFIN
LOW-FAT	

```
C A N N E D M W J K N I P K
E N L H C T A C Y F H H H J
E I M B A I F A I S B E U B
G E I F A R H S U L L N I T
R T W I E C H S U P A G I S
A O S S N E O E E E E N A S
L R H H R O F R C Y W N T T
Y P E I T I I O E A D N Y A
E R E N N S A L T W A T E R
N S U G W S M E I R E L L K
I E A C A T R C U I B E L I
R A W L R A H A D O K M O S
A F M K A E T S A N U T W T
M O H J S S M T E L L I F H
N O V N E T S Y G O L O I B
I D M R H I D O L P H I N S
```

Solution on Page 361

BLUE MARTINI

BLUSH

CATHOUSE

COYOTE UGLY

ESPN ZONE

EYE CANDY

GHOSTBAR

GOLD DIGGERS

I BAR

JET

KRAVE

LAVO

MIX

NOIR BAR

OCTANE

POETRY

PURE

PUSSYCAT DOLLS

RAIN LAS VEGAS

RISQUE

ROCKHOUSE

ROK

RUM JUNGLE

SEAMLESS

TABU

TAO

TRIQ

VOODOO LOUNGE

WASTED SPACE

```
E T S L Y V F H Z J C U Q M
E G D R R O C K H O U S E W
S C N A E U S T E N A T C O
W A A U R G M E D U W T A C
D E G P O A G J A P L I T I
D I M E S L B I U M I X H R
H G C M V D O R D N L T O A
U E H O N S E O I D G E U B
P U S S Y C A T D O L L S T
N Q U P K O R L S O N O E S
Q S L P N A T S N A O E G O
Q I B O M Z I E Q I W V N H
Y R R E R B O K U B A A A G
H R U T A B U N W G T R F L
X L M R U L P B E B L K E O
B Z I Y E Y E C A N D Y T R
```

Solution on Page 361

APRON	PAJAMAS
BANDANNA	PANTSUIT
BLAZER	RAINCOAT
BLOUSE	RAYON
BOOT	SCARF
BOW TIE	SHORTS
BUTTONS	SILK
COLLAR	SKIRTS
CORDUROY	SLACKS
COTTON	SLEEVE
CUFFS	SOCKS
DRESS	SWEATER
FROCK	TAILOR
GLOVES	TIGHTS
JACKET	TROUSERS
JEANS	TUNIC
JERSEY	TWEED
JUMPSUIT	VEST
KHAKIS	WOOL
OVERCOAT	ZIPPER

```
S K C O S R J E S U O L B Y
E J S L A C K S E V O L G C
D E A Y J A C K E T O O B U R
R A O U P C B R U Y L I R F
E N N R I U C C O T T O N F
S S O N T O T R O U S E R S
S N U T A J U M P S U I T Q
Z T O T A D L Z S C A R F T
L N R B R O N P I I N R R S
S S T O O R C A A P L D O E
I T C W H Y E N B J P K C V
K H O T E S E T I L A E K E
A G L I Q E W S A A A M R E
H I L E Z Z D U R E R Z A L
K T A I L O R I K E W B E S
R Y R S K I R T S S J S J R
```

Solution on Page 361

AERODYNAMIC

AIR PRESSURE

ANTI-ROLL BAR

BLACK FLAG

BLUE FLAG

BODYWORK

BRAKES

BUMP

CARBON FIBER

CASTER

CHASSIS

CHECKERED FLAG

COMPOUND

DIFFUSER

DRAFTING

DRIVER

FLAGS

HELMET

HORSEPOWER

LINE

OPEN WHEEL

PITS

QUALIFYING

REBOUND

RED FLAG

SLICKS

STEERING WHEEL

TETHER

TORQUE

TRANSPONDER

TUNNELS

```
S T E E R I N G W H E E L P
G N I Y F I L A U Q K R I M
N B L A C K F L A G S T W U
I L B O I D I F F U S E R B
T U Q A E R O D Y N A M I C
F E T C D O P E N W H E E L
A F U A N T I R O L L B A R
R L N R U R S E E N I L J C
D A N B O E L K V S V P A P
R G E O P B I C H A S S I S
E T L N M O C E H D T U D W
H O S F O U K H S E K A R B
T R Y I C N S C R Z L I I E
E Q H B O D Y W O R K M V F
T U R E W O P E S R O H E W
L E T R A N S P O N D E R T
```

Solution on Page 362

ART

BATHROOM

CEILING

CEMENT

CERAMIC

COLOR

DECORATIVE

DESIGNER

FLAT

FLOORING

GLAZED

GLUE

GRANITE

GROUT

HARD

KITCHEN

LAY

LIMESTONE

MARBLE

METAL

MORTAR

MOSAICS

PATTERNS

PLASTIC

PORCELAIN

QUARRY

ROOFS

SAW

SHOWERS

SLATE

SQUARE

WALLS

WATER

WHITE

WOOD

```
W  I  M  O  R  T  A  R  O  L  O  C  A  Y
K  R  O  O  F  S  E  G  F  L  A  T  W  H
U  L  K  O  S  S  R  E  W  O  H  S  E  A
Q  O  D  Q  U  A  R  R  Y  W  A  T  E  R
K  G  R  E  N  G  I  S  E  D  A  T  F  D
J  I  U  I  C  D  G  C  S  L  I  C  G  M
B  A  T  H  R  O  O  M  S  H  H  E  L  Q
S  E  N  C  P  F  R  O  W  A  N  R  A  P
Q  C  T  I  H  L  P  A  W  O  W  A  Z  S
U  G  T  R  A  E  A  A  T  N  E  M  E  C
A  M  E  T  A  L  N  S  T  I  L  I  D  R
R  G  N  I  L  I  E  C  T  T  V  C  J  X
E  L  B  R  A  M  J  C  F  I  E  E  F  Z
J  U  L  F  I  T  U  O  R  G  C  R  O  T
W  A  L  L  S  C  F  L  O  O  R  I  N  G
Y  N  F  G  S  L  J  C  N  F  P  B  Y  S
```

Solution on Page 362

ACTOR

ALBUM

ARMY

ARTIST

BLUE SUEDE

COLONEL

CONCERT

COUNTRY

DANCE

FAMOUS

GOSPEL

GRACELAND

GRAMMYS

GUITAR

HAIR

HAWAII

HIPS

HOUND DOG

ICON

IDOL

JUMPSUIT

LAS VEGAS

LEATHER

LISA MARIE

MEMPHIS

MOVIES

MUSICIAN

PERFORMER

POPULAR

PRISCILLA

RECORDS

ROCK

SIDEBURNS

SINGER

SONGS

STAR

TENNESSEE

THE KING

TOUR

TUPELO

```
G Y N O C I J P G U I T A R
S M M Y R T N U O C R I L C
Y R E C O R D S M P N D B O
M A M B A C T O R P U O U N
M P P L A S V E G A S L M C
A E H U H I P S G A T U A E
R R I E E K C O R R C S I R
G F S S I B I R A T O O N T
O O I U P R I S C I L L A H
S R D E O A A K E S O E I E
P M E D H M W M L T N P C K
E E B E N K A W A D E U I I
L R U O T U H F N S L T S N
M L R S G N O S D N I T U G
S I N G E R E H T A E L M B
E E S S E N N E T D A N C E
```

Solution on Page 362

BARS	FORMAL
BEER	FRANCHISE
BUSBOY	HOSTESS
CASUAL	ITALIAN
CHEFS	LINE COOK
CHINESE	LUNCH
COOKS	MANAGER
CRITIC	MEALS
CUISINE	MENUS
CULINARY	OWNER
CULTURE	PORTIONS
DECOR	REVIEWS
DESSERT	SEAFOOD
DINING	SERVICE
DISHES	SOUP
EATING	SPECIAL
ENTREE	TAVERNS
ETHNIC	WAITERS
FAST FOOD	WATER
FOOD SAFETY	WINE

```
E E R T N E L A I C E P S I
B W R E V I E W S C H E F S
U A A U D A D I N I N G Y N
S I R T T I W M A N A G E R
B T G S E L S I B H I S D E
O E F N O R U H N T L S E V
Y R A N I L U C E E A E S A
S S P O R T I O N S T T S T
R L S N F R A N C H I S E U
D L A U S A C E E R E O R T
L O S E N I S I U C I H T L
A W O O M E W T I B O T Q U
M N U F N R M V F B E O I N
R E P I A E R C O O K S K C
O R H Y T E F A S D O O F H
F C U T S B S R O C E D U S
```

Solution on Page 362

AGATE	PLAY
AGGIE	POCKET
ALLEY	QUITSIES
BALL	RINGER
CAT'S EYE	ROLLING
CHILDREN	ROUND
CIRCLE	SHOOTER
CLAY	SIZE
COLLECTING	SMALL
COLORS	SPHERICAL
DESIGN	STEEL
DIRT	STONE
FLICK	SWIRL
FOR KEEPS	TAKE
GAMES	TARGET
GLASS	THUMB
HIT	TOYS
KEEPSIES	TRADE
LOSE	WIN
NOSTALGIA	

Marbles

```
N G I S E D N U O R T U U Y
T P T E K C O P E I G G A P
O N R I S I R S H N G G L Z
Y H I S L M E T A G A A L X
S A D P P R A L L E Y E E X
E Q S E C H I L D R E N X E
M P E E N L E W L T G S H W
A I I K Y O A R S N Q T E I
G Q S I Z E S Y I R O O K C
L N T P T J S T E C T N A S
A I I H E R C T A R A E T G
S W U L O E O F A L L L E H
S M Q L L O K D R C G S G S
B A O L H O E R R E O I R F
M C O S V K R I O L L L A B
Q C R F L I C K J F O X T U
```

Solution on Page 363

ALCOHOL	LIEBFRAUMILCH
BORDEAUX	MADEIRA
BORDELAIS	MOSEL
CHAMPAGNE	MUSCATEL
CHENIN BLANC	PINOT NOIR
CHIANTI	RESIDUAL SUGAR
COLD DUCK	RHINE
CONSUMPTION	RIOJA
DANDELION	SONOMA COUNTY
DESSERT WINE	WINE FESTIVALS
ELDERBERRY	WINE TOURISM
FERMENT	WINEMAKING
FORTIFIED	
JUG	

Wine Tour

```
G U J Y R R E B R E D L E G
N A Y T N U O C A M O N O S
I R C H A M P A G N E X C R
K L I E B F R A U M I L C H
A L C O H O L C S O B B L I
M D N D N F R H L S O O E N
E E A E D T M I A E R R T E
N I L S F A O A U L D D A G
I F B S D Z E N D G E E C C
W I N E F E S T I V A L S O
P T I R H E Z I S P U A U L
N R N T N E M R E F X I M D
A O E W A J O I R F R S K D
R F H I D A N D E L I O N U
A J C N O I T P M U S N O C
W I N E T O U R I S M Z T K
```

Solution on Page 363

ANALYZE

BIOLOGY

CHEMISTRY

CONCLUSION

CONTROL

DATA

EMPIRICAL

EXPERIMENT

HYPOTHESIS

INQUIRY

KNOWLEDGE

LAB

LOGIC

MEASURABLE

METHOD

MODEL

OBJECTIVE

OBSERVE

PHENOMENA

PREDICTION

PROCEDURE

QUESTION

REACTION

REASONING

RESEARCH

RESULTS

RETEST

SCIENTISTS

STEPS

TECHNIQUES

THEORIES

The Scientific Method

```
S T L U S E R E S E A R C H
E V I T C E J B O P T U H T
G N I N O S A E R H A S E I
D P R O C E D U R E D C M N
E M P I R I C A L N N I I Q
L O R T N O C R S O M E S U
W S E E X P E R I M E N T I
O E D J R T Q S S E A T R R
N U I L E L U L E N S I Y Y
K Q C S A L E A H A U S G E
D I T B C O S N T L R T O V
O N I N T G T A O E A S L R
H H O W I I I L P D B T O E
T C N P O C O Y Y O L E I S
E E B S N X N Z H M E P B B
M T H E O R I E S J F S Y O
```

Solution on Page 363

ARREST	LIEUTENANT
ARSON	MOTOR OFFICER
BADGE	NARCOTICS
BATON	NIGHTSTICK
BUST	NYPD
CANINE	PARTNER
COMMISSIONER	POLICE CAR
DETECTIVE	PROTECT
DISPATCHER	SECURITY
DRAGNET	SERGEANT
DUTY	SIREN
ENFORCEMENT	SUSPECT
FLARE	SWAT
FORENSICS	TICKET
GANG	VICTIM
HANDCUFFS	WARRANT
HORSEBACK	
LAPD	

Police

```
D S D V S P P E Y N O C G K
R E C I F F O R O T O M C T
A R A C S G F T O M U A M N
G G N T V P A U M T B D I A
N E I I W B A I C E E G S N
E A N M B U S T S D H C Y E
T N E R I S P R C T N T T T
T T F V I A O A S H I A E U
S C G O I H L T R R E K H E
E G N J R T I T U T C R G I
R E A N A C C C C I N D M L
R P G W K Y E E T E A E D A
A R S O N S C M T B P P R P
W T N A R R A W E E Y S Y D
S C I S N E R O F N D E U C
F L A R E N A R C O T I C S
```

Solution on Page 363

ALLOWANCE

BABY

BIRTH

CAREGIVER

CHILDREN

CHORES

DAD

DAUGHTER

DISCIPLINE

FAMILY

FATHER

GUARDIAN

JOY

LOVE

MATERNAL

MOM

MOTHER

NANNY

NURTURE

PARENT

PATIENCE

PREGNANCY

PRIDE

RESPONSIBILITY

SON

```
E N C Y B A L L O W A N C E E
T I L J Z C I P H N A N N Y
R R E V M F R W B S A I I O
R E S P O N S I B I L I T Y
K T N F T B U R D P R I D E
O H C A H L V R I Y K T U C
B G N T E S A C T P N L H U
E U E H R U S N R U A O J T
C A R E G I V E R G R V I W
N D D R D Y G H M E S E Q L
E D L Z B N E Y S O T P D F
I Z I J A T H Y L I M A F N
T I H N B D L H O S D R M W
A B C T Y Y K Z G J O E O Q
P Y L S U S B F Z O X N I S
N E O U K W T J E B M T S Z
```

Solution on Page 364

ABALONE

BACTERIA

BALEEN

BARRACUDA

CARP

CEPHALOPODS

CLAMS

COPEPODS

CORAL

CRAPPIE

CRUSTACEAN

CUTTLEFISH

EEL

FLOUNDER

FLUKE

GOBY

GOLDFISH

GUPPY

HUMPBACK

JELLYFISH

KELP

LOBSTER

MACKEREL

MINNOW

MUSSEL

NAUTILUS

ORANGE ROUGHY

PORPOISE

SCALLOPS

SCAVENGER

SEA TURTLES

SEAHORSE

SOLE

YELLOWTAIL

```
D Y P P U G O L D F I S H T
F B A C T E R I A L X S Y P
C L E R E K C A M O K C R H
Y R A Z S E L T R U T A E S
C H A R D L A W S N C V N I
A U G P O P M O U D N E O F
K D T U P C S L L E A N L Y
C P U T O I K L I R E G A L
A O S C L R E E T G C E B L
B R P N A E E Y U O A R A E
P P O E H R F G A B T E M J
M O L E P S R I N Y S T I E
U I L L E O O A S A U S N K
H S A A C O D L B H R B N U
X E C B M U S S E L C O O L
O E S R O H A E S E E L W F
```

Solution on Page 364

ALLSPICE

ANISE

BAY LEAF

CARAWAY

CARDAMOM

CELERY SEED

CHERVIL

CHILI POWDER

CHILI SAUCE

CHIVES

CINNAMON

CLOVES

CORIANDER

CUMIN

DILL

FENNEL

HEMP

HOREHOUND

LICORICE

LIVERWORT

MACE

MANDRAKE

MONKSHOOD

NUTMEG

PAPRIKA

PARSLEY

POPPY SEED

RELISH

SALT

SESAME SEED

SPEARMINT

TARRAGON

THYME

WINTERGREEN

```
E E C I P S L L A S A L T C
S C C T R O W R E V I L H M
E P I U R S P A R S L E Y O
V A E R A E E P K N R W M M
O D K A O S L V Y V H I E A
L Q N I R C I I I S D N A D
C Q U U R M I L S H E T E R
R E D W O P I L I H C E D A
M E L O N H A N F H S R D C
A B D E O O E P T E C G C I
N N A N R H G R M M E R A N
D U I Y A Y S A O P S E R N
R T D M L I S K R H I E A A
A M I A U E R E N R N N W M
K E L C S C A O E O A C A O
E G L E N N E F C D M T Y N
```

Solution on Page 364

AIRTIGHT	PACKAGING
BEANS	PICK
BOILING	PRESERVING
CANNER	PRESSURE
COOK	PROCESSED
FACTORY	QUART
FISH	RING
FOODS	SALT
FRESH	SEALED
FRUITS	SHELF LIFE
HOME	SOUP
INDUSTRY	STORAGE
JARS	TIN
JELLY	TOMATOES
LIDS	TUNA
MASON JAR	VACUUM
MEAT	VEGETABLES
METAL	WATER

```
F Y C Z S B M B Q B P U O S
A O O N N H O M E T R A U Q
W U O G N I V R E S E R P G
R A K D L W T V H E S A I D
A I T I S T A E M V S J C F
A O N E T E L G D A U N K I
Q G Y G R F O E E C R O H S
S X P N L N D T L U E S N H
T H G I T R I A A U J A R S
I R F G N K W B E M E M N A
U E R A S D I L S B O A D R
R N E K C Y U E K M E T A L
F N S C D E S S E C O R P H
H A H A G F A C T O R Y F P
A C P P G L E G A R O T S G
F A N U T R J E L L Y L S U
```

Solution on Page 364

ALDER	HIMALAYAN
APRICOT	HOLLY
ASH	LILAC
BEECH	LOCUST
BIRCH	MAGNOLIA
BUCKEYE	MAPLE
CEDAR	MULBERRY
CHERRY	OAK
CHESTNUT	OLIVE
COTTONWOOD	PALM
CYPRESS	PEACH
DATE	PECAN
DOGWOOD	PINE
ELM	PLUM
EUCALYPTUS	POPLAR
FIR	SPRUCE
HAWTHORN	WALNUT
HICKORY	WILLOW

Trees

```
R X D O Y R H H U C A L I L
W P O P L A R O Y B C X X G
V I G Y E X L P I H S B N N
L D W B L Y R R E B L U M A
C A O J C E C S P R U C E C
D E O O S H T B B E S K X E
C T D S W N K A N D U E V P
Y Y F A U N A R D L T Y W E
E R I T R E O Y W A P E V A
B O R Y O H W T A I Y I K C
V K G E T C S A T L L E N H
J C M W H V I A L O A L F E
F I A U O C S R C N C M O Z
R H P A L M E U P G U M I W
P Y L Q L P S E I A E T W H
E S E U Y T M U B M U S Z G
```

Solution on Page 365

PUZZLES • 303

AIR RIFLES	KIDDIE RIDES
ARCADE	MERRY-GO-ROUND
BAKED GOODS	PINK LEMONADE
BOUNCY	RACES
BUMPER CARS	ROLLER COASTER
COIN TOSS	SHOWS
COMPETITIONS	SNOW CONES
FERRIS WHEEL	STAGE
FLEA MARKETS	SWINGING SHIP
FOOD	THRILL RIDES
FRIED CHICKEN	TILT-A-WHIRL
FUNFAIR	WATER RIDES
HANDICRAFTS	

```
M S N O I T I T E P M O C L
L E E H W S I R R E F C N T
R D R Y C N U O B L C K T H
I I A R C A D E E S I S N R
H R R O Y Y E A E D T S E I
W R A I I G M N D F W T K L
A E C I A A O I A I S S C L
T T E T R C E R N A C D I R
L A S K W R C G O Z O O H I
I W E O I I I C M U I O C D
T T N D D N R F E R N G D E
S S E N G E W O L R T D E S
E S A S L G O O K E O E I H
I H H L E Z R D N G S K R O
T I O F U N F A I R S A F W
P R S R A C R E P M U B R S
```

Solution on Page 365

BILLION	QUADRILLION
DECILLION	QUINTILLION
EIGHTEEN	SEPTILLION
EIGHTY	SEVENTEEN
ELEVEN	SEVENTY
FIFTEEN	SEXTILLION
FIFTY	SIXTEEN
FIVE	SIXTY
FORTY	TEN
FOURTEEN	THIRTEEN
GOOGOL	THIRTY
HUNDRED	THOUSAND
MILLION	THREE
NINETEEN	TRILLION
NINETY	TWELVE
NONILLION	TWENTY
OCTILLION	TWO
ONE	

```
L Z Z T F N E E T X I S Z C
F O J M W I E I G H T Y Y N
O S G A N E V E L E S X T I
U N D O N E N E T E N V X N
R N O N O O E T X F O F I E
T Y O I A G I T Y D I I S T
E T A I L S I L E C L F E Y
E R H Y L L U C L N L T V T
N O N I L L I O N I I Y E N
E F B I R L I R H Q T N N E
E F O I L T E R D T N P T V
T N T I L V Y P T A I V E E
H N O I L L I T C O U D E S
G N E E T R I H T E Q Q N R
I T W O G E N O I L L I M X
E T H R E E H U N D R E D I
```

Solution on Page 365

AIR FILTER	FUSES
ALTERNATOR	GASKETS
ANTENNA	HEADLIGHTS
BEARINGS	HOSES
BRAKES	OIL CHANGE
BUCKET SEAT	PAINT
CHOKE	PARKING LIGHT
CLUTCH PLATE	TACHOMETER
CV JOINT	TIMING CHAIN
DOORS	VALVES
ELECTRICAL	WATER PUMP
ENGINE PARTS	WINDSHIELD
FUEL INJECTION	WIPER MOTOR
FUEL PUMP	

```
F U S E S R E T L I F R I A
S N I S T H G I L D A E H L
R O W I P E R M O T O R L T
O I O B E A R I N G S G L E
O T H G I L G N I K R A P R
D C A O S E E G Z O C S O N
L E L N S E X C F L V K O A
E J K U N E K H T W J E I T
I N P O T E S A T R O T L O
H I A A H C T I R H I S C R
S L I R I C H N O B N C H V
D E N G I N E P A R T S A A
N U T A P M U P L E U F N L
I F P M U P R E T A W U G V
W B U C K E T S E A T H E E
T W W T A C H O M E T E R S
```

Solution on Page 365

ATTACK

BISHOPS

BLACK

BOARD GAME

CAPTURE

CASTLING

CHAMPION

CHECKERED

CHECKMATE

CHESSBOARD

CLUB

COMPUTER

FORK

FUN

GAMBIT

KINGS

KNIGHTS

MASTERS

MOVES

OPPONENT

PAWNS

PIECES

QUEEN

ROOKS

RULES

SKILL

SQUARES

STALEMATE

STRATEGY

TACTICS

THINKING

TURN

WHITE

WIN

The Game of Kings

```
B O A R D G A M E R P N T O
C A P T U R E E I W I N A O
F B L N E T A M K C E H C A
P A W N S E V O M C C E T J
X S S P O H S I B A E T I D
A C M A S T E R S S S A C E
T E T I H W C K S T S M S R
T K V G K R O F K L E E H E
A I I V U O M R O I R L H K
C N C H A M P I O N A A K C
K G B H N J U P R G U T G E
Z S S L Q E T E O J Q S A H
N S T R A T E G Y N S R M C
R U L E S C R U H N E E B L
U R Z L L I K S Q F U N I U
T U S C U G N I K N I H T B
```

Solution on Page 366

ANDREWS	LOREN
BANCROFT	MACLAINE
BATES	MATLIN
BERGMAN	MIRREN
BERRY	PALTROW
CHER	REDGRAVE
CRAWFORD	ROBERTS
DAVIS	SARANDON
DUNAWAY	SPACEK
FIELDS	STREEP
FLETCHER	STREISAND
FONDA	SWANK
FOSTER	TANDY
HEPBURN	TAYLOR
HUNT	THERON
KEATON	THOMPSON
KELLY	WINSLET
KIDMAN	WITHERSPOON
LANGE	WYMAN

Best Actress

```
R O B E R T S I V A D P V N
Y L L E K Q F O N D A Q U O
J M I R R E N O D N A R A S
E G N A L G C A S T R E E P
T N I L T A M A M T A D B M
G S W O R T L A P Y E G E O
D Z T N U H F Y N S W R R H
U O C R A W F O R D F A R T
N R H H E P B U R N R V Y H
A F Z T K I R E H C T E L F
W I T H E R S P O O N T W B
A E N I A L C A M P O A L S
Y L B A T E S I N E R Y B W
Y D X L O R E N B D E L N A
K S N A N A M D I K H O X N
R Y D N A T U A M W T R Q K
```

Solution on Page 366

PUZZLES • 313

ASPHALT	PEAKED
BUILDING	PITCH
CHIMNEY	PROTECTS
COLLAPSE	REPAIR
COVERING	REPLACE
DRAINAGE	ROOFER
DURABILITY	SHINGLES
DWELLING	SLATE
EAVES	SLOPE
FELT	SNOW
FLAT	SOLAR
GABLE	STRAW
GUTTERS	TAR
HOUSE	THATCHING
INSULATION	TILES
MATERIAL	TOP
METAL	WEATHER
NAILS	WOOD

Roofs

```
T A L F G D T B A L W O O D
I T F O Y E N M I H C G B E
L L A I R E T A M O N W U K
E A V E S G R O V I O M I A
S H V Y N A S E H G A B L E
W P S C T N R C W J J E D P
A S H N O I T A L U S N I I
R A I W N A L N L P Q L N T
T O N G H R J I A O J L G C
S C G T L D W L B I S N C H
L R L P T E L E C A L P E R
A L E O A O P R Z L R S E E
T A S T C E T O R P T U P P
E T H R T G N I L L E W D A
U E A H O U S E E S S H S I
R M Q S V C G F R O O F E R
```

Solution on Page 366

ACADEMIC

AUTHORITY

CAMPAIGNS

CANDIDATES

CHANGE

CITIZEN

CORPORATE

CORRUPTION

DECISIONS

DEMOCRAT

ECONOMY

ELECTIONS

EXECUTIVE

FEDERAL

GOVERNMENT

GROUP

HOUSE

LAWS

MAJORITY

MILITARY

NATIONAL

PARLIAMENT

PLATFORM

POLITICIAN

POWER

PRESIDENT

PUBLIC

REVOLUTION

STATE

TAXES

VOTING

```
E A C A D E M I C I L B U P
V C L A W S N O I T C E L E
I H C Y N C A M P A I G N S
T A T M N O L A N O I T A N
U N N P I O I D S E X A T L
C G E P O L I T I C I A N A
E E M M B D I T U V P S H R
X P N E A U E T P L U C O E
E R R T U I G C A U O T U D
C E E A T A L T I R R V S E
O S V T H V F R P S Y R E F
N I O S O O W O A O I L O R
O D G T R G R O U P W O M C
M E I M I A C I T I Z E N Z
Y N P R T A R C O M E D R S
G T C E Y T I R O J A M U M
```

Solution on Page 366

ALARM	MILITARY
ANALOG	MINUTES
ASTRONOMY	MONTH
ATOMIC	NOON
BATTERY	PENDULUM
BELL	QUARTZ
BIG BEN	ROUND
CUCKOO	SECONDS
DAY	SETTING
DECORATIVE	SOLAR
DIGITAL	SUNDIAL
DISPLAY	TICK
ELECTRIC	TIMEPIECE
FACE	TOWER
HANDS	TRAVEL
HOURGLASS	WALL
INSTRUMENT	WATCHES
INVENTION	WIND
LATE	YEAR
METRONOME	

Telling Time

```
Y H D I G I T A L E V A R T
D A N N P Y A L P S I D A O
N N U V B M D C L F U T L W
I D O E I O G I K E O K A E
W S R N G N O R C M B E R R
A E T T B O L T I O M S M A
L T I I E R A C T N U E S L
L U M O N T N E L O L C E O
R N E N S S A L G R U O H S
A I P X L A T E Z T D N C Z
E M I L I T A R Y E N D T F
Y R E T T A B A U M E S A N
C U C K O O D M C M P C W O
U N E V I T A R O C E D H O
L A I D N U S E T T I N G N
M O N T H S Q R Q U A R T Z
```

Solution on Page 367

PUZZLES • **319**

ANIMATORS	FUN
AWARDS	GRAPHICS
BUG'S LIFE	HOLLYWOOD
CALIFORNIA	LAMP
CARS	MONSTERS
CARTOON	MOVIES
CGI	NEMO
CHARACTERS	RELEASE
COMPANY	SHORTS
COMPUTER	STEVE JOBS
DIGITAL	STUDIO
DISNEY	SUCCESS
FAMILY	TECHNOLOGY
FEATURE	TOY STORY
FILMS	WALL-E

```
R M O V I E S C I H P A R G
F D S S S E C C U S I E W S
R I G C A R T O O N U F A M
O N O L K Q Z F R M K I L L
I S T E V E J O B S P R L I
D R S F F C F E R U T A E F
U A R A N I M A T O R S N G
T C E Y L D L A W A R D S Y
S R T A R N O S F V J I S E
T E C H N O L O G Y U G R N
R L A M P N T P W U D I E S
O E R V P E D S Z Y B T T I
H A A F A M I L Y F L A S D
S S H T P O L Q A O M L N I
O E C O M P U T E R T Q O V
Z T E U H V T T F X M R M H
```

Solution on Page 367

AIDES

ANESTHETICS

ANTIBIOTIC

BEDPAN

BIRTHING ROOM

BLOOD

CARDIOLOGY

CLINIC

DELIVERY ROOM

DIETICIAN

DRUG

EMERGENCY

EXAMINING ROOM

GERIATRICS

INTENSIVE CARE

MAINTENANCE

OPERATION

ORDERLY

PRIVATE ROOM

RECORDS

RECOVERY ROOM

TRANSFUSION

TRAUMA ROOM

VITAL SIGNS

WARDS

WINGS

Hospital

```
D H Z P Y G O L O I D R A C
S C I R T A I R E G M B X L
S N G I S L A T I V O T L D
I A Y V A N T I B I O T I C
B N U A T R A U M A R O O M
I E T T O R D E R L Y G D C
R S D E L I V E R Y R O O M
T T I R N O I T A R E P O Y
H H E O G S E D I A V B L C
I E T O U W I N G S O E B N
N T I M R S S V R P C D N E
G I C S D R O C E R E P U G
R C I R C L I N I C R A U R
O S A M A I N T E N A N C E
O W N O I S U F S N A R T M
M O O R G N I N I M A X E E
```

Solution on Page 367

ALPS	MILK RUN
ASPEN	MOGULS
BADGER PASS	OFF TRAILS
BASE	PARK CITY
BINDINGS	POWDER
BLACK DIAMONDS	RESORT
BUNNY SLOPE	RUNS
CATCHING AIR	SCHUSSING
DOWNHILL	SKIS
FALL LINE	SNOWBOARD
FREESTYLE	SUN VALLEY
INSTRUCTOR	SUNGLASSES
JACKSON HOLE	TELLURIDE
LAKE TAHOE	VAIL
LIFT	WINTER
MAGIC MOUNTAIN	

```
S N O W B O A R D M F I R I K
K T E O H A T E K A L P U S I
I E V B N E P S A G L O N E S
S L F A B M T O L I I W S S S
R Y P D I I E R P C H D L S S
N T A G N L L T S M N E I A T
T S R E D K L L P O W R A L F
F E K R I R U G M U O O R G A
A E C P N U R A L N D T T N E
L R I A G N I H C T A C F U L
L F T S S D D E S A B U F S L
L T Y S K R E T N I W R O L I
I F S C H U S S I N G T M U N
N I A Y E L L A V N U S M G E
E L O H N O S K C A J N Z O B
B U N N Y S L O P E Y I J M
```

Solution on Page 367

Answers

Broadway Musicals

Bank Terms

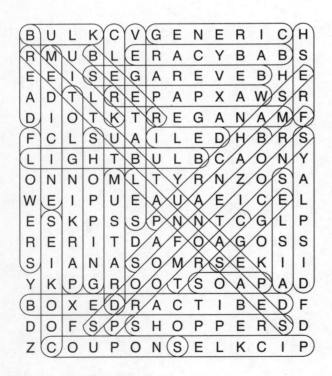

Grocery Store

Pastry

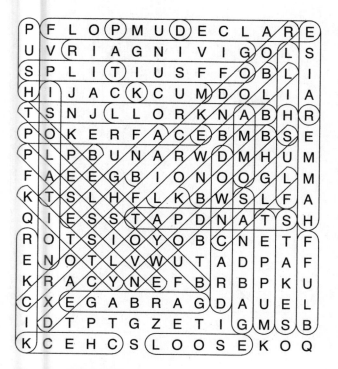

Play Poker

Fun in the Pool

At School

Botany

Hewlett-Packard

The Big Apple

Countries

Classic Arcade Games

Board Games

Numismatics

Camp Out

College Life

Family Barbecue

Treats

Trading Cards

Easter

European Vacation

Go Golf

Delicatessen

Musicians

Health

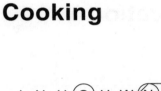

Cooking

Lawn Care

Movers and Shakers

334

Literary

Rock Climbing

DVD

Gardening

In the Stars

Arboretum

Gene Study

Insects

Cocktails

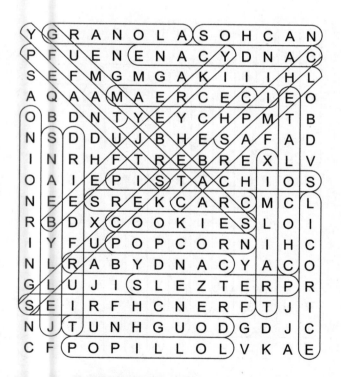

Late-Night Snacks

First Ladies

Juggling

Caffeine

Digital Photography

Felines

St. Louis

338

Lunar Eclipse

Bankable

Rainforests

It's Legal

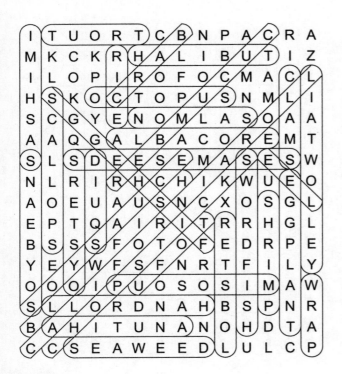

Sushi

Going to School

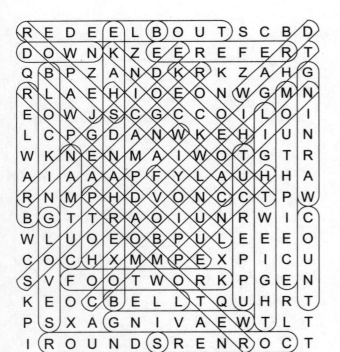

Boxing

School Supplies

340

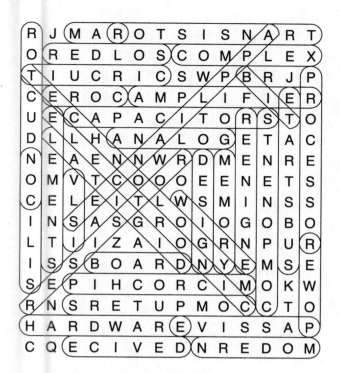

Integrated Circuits

Chemicals

Classic TV

Disneyland

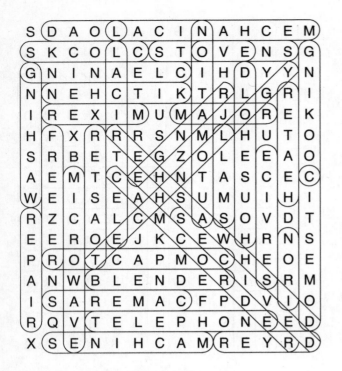

Home Appliance

Emotions

Kitchen Utensils

Studying Plants

342

Humor Me

On Television

Sewing Circle

Penny

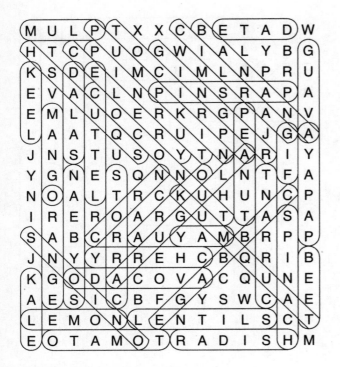

Healthy Foods

Medicine

Mapmaking

Intoxicating

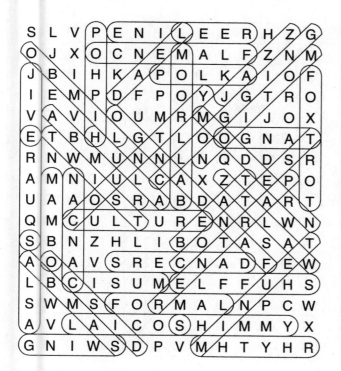

Dance Time

Edible Seeds

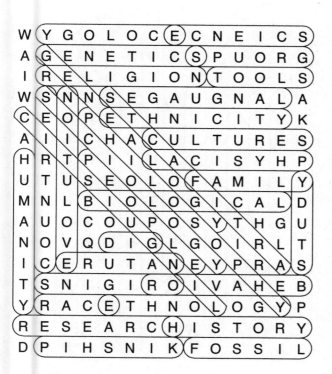

Anthropology

Outdoor Adventure

Jellyfish

Get Around

Bonsai

Business Names

346

Cartoons

Christmastime

Cookies

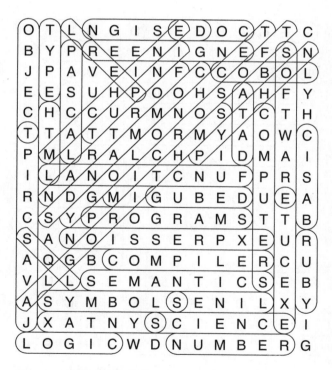

Programming Languages

Around the Kitchen

Big Cities

Family Tree

Cork

348

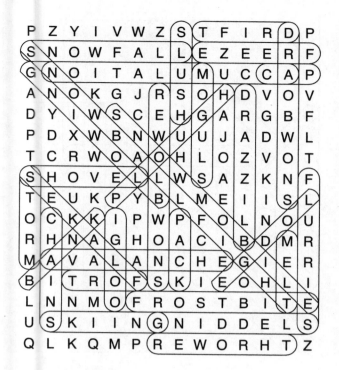

Let It Snow

On the Calendar

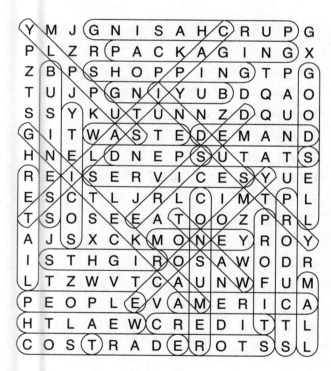

Consumerism

County Fairs

Street Names

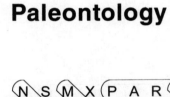

Paleontology

Engineering

Jazz and Swing

Exercise

Photography

Siblings

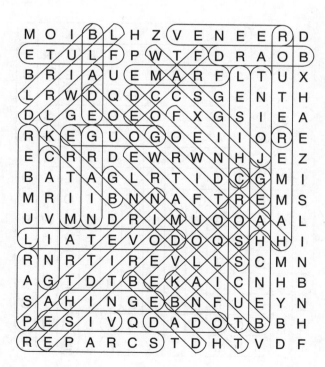

Woodworking

Science World

Speaking of Horses

Social Networks

Baby Names

Collectibles

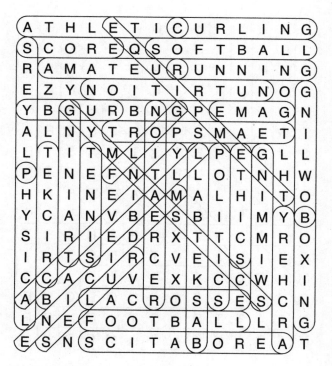

Plumbing

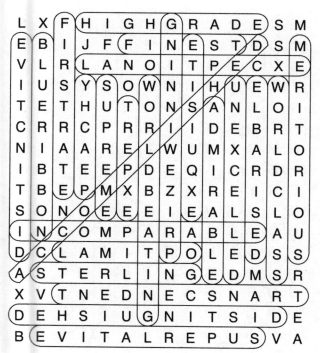

Good Words

Sporting Chance

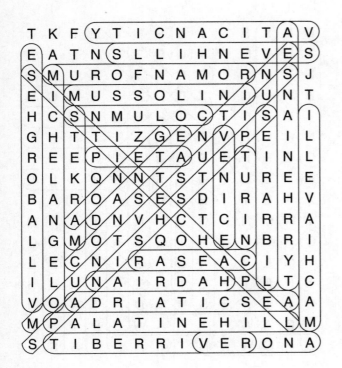

Italian

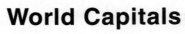

World Capitals

Take a Trip

Zoo

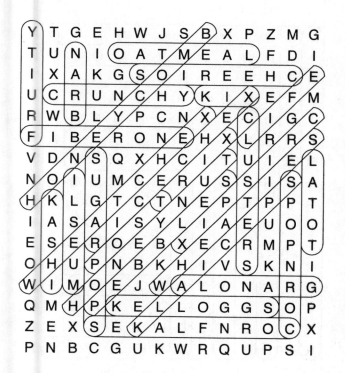

Breakfast Cereals

Child Development

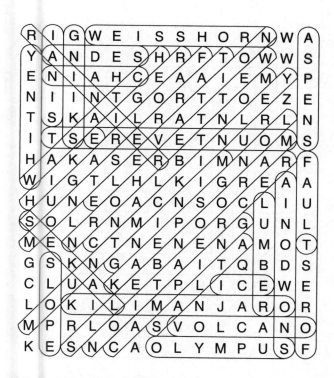

Mountain View

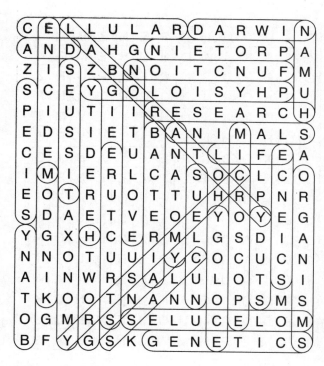

Biology

Salad Toppings

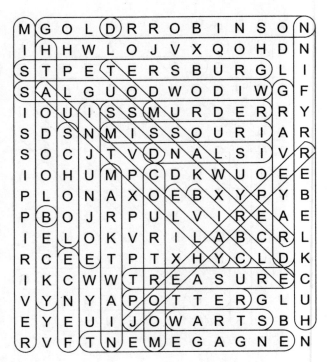

The Adventures of Tom Sawyer

Baseball

Real Estate

356

New England

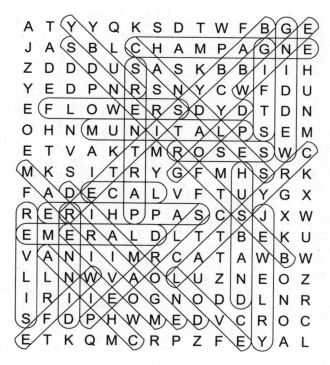

The Las Vegas Strip

State Capitals

Wedding Anniversary

Basic Words

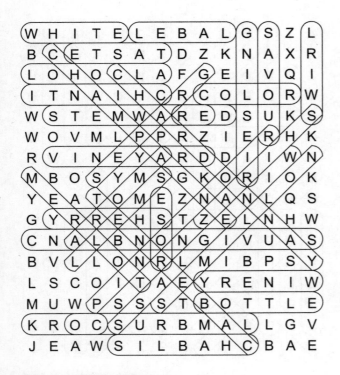

Wine Tasting

Latin

High School Graduation

358

Watch It

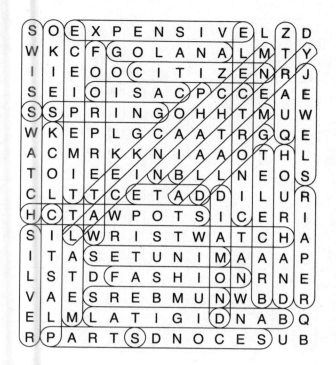

Health Provider

Pigs

Furniture Types

The Old Man and the Sea

Toss a Salad

Model Rocket

Whoopi Goldberg

National Parks

```
K O B U K V A L L E Y M R L
S E D A C S A C H T R O N F
F E E R L O T I P A C U O I
P L F E B P C I I K A N Y K
A R I D I X O A Y A N T N E
D E R W G P L M R R A R A N
R W E O B O O T R C V A C A
E O I O E U N A E H E I N I
I T S D N S I K F E R N E F
S L T D H A B S S A I L   J
L L A K E C L A R K L E G O
A I N O Y N A C E C Y R B R
N V D J D O C E P A C Z Y D
D E I D R Y T O R T U G A S
X D D E A T H V A L L E Y J
W D E E R T A U H S O J S F
```

Tuna

```
C A N N E D M W J K N I P K
E N L H C T A C Y F H H H J
E I M B A I F A I S B E U B
G E I F A R H S U L L N I T
R T W I E C H S U P A G I S
A O S S N E O E E E E N A S
L R H H R O F R C Y W N T T
Y P E I T I I O E A D N Y A
E R E N N S A L T W A T E R
N S U G W S M E I R E L L K
I E A C A T R C U I B E L I
R A W L R A H A D O K M O S
A F M K A E T S A N U T W T
M O H J S S M T E L L I F H
N O V N E T S Y G O L O I B
I D M R H I D O L P H I N S
```

Nightlife

```
E T S L Y V F H Z J C U Q M
E G D R R O C K H O U S E W
S C N A E U S T E N A T C O
W A A U R G M E D U W T A C
D E G P O A G J A P L I T I
D I M E S L B I U M I X H R
H G C M V D O R D N L T O A
U E H O N S E O I D G E U B
P U S S Y C A T D O L L S T
N Q U P K O R L S O N O E S
Q S L P N A T S N A O E G O
Q I B O M Z I E Q I W V N H
Y R R E R B O K U B A A A G
H R U T A B U N W G T R F L
X L M R U L P B E B L K E O
B Z I Y E Y E C A N D Y T R
```

Wear It Well

```
S K C O S R J E S U O L B Y
E J S L A C K S E V O L G C
D E A Y J A C K E T O O B U
R A O U P C B R U Y L I R F
E N N R I U C C O T T O N F
S S O N T O T R O U S E R S
S N U T A J U M P S U I T Q
Z T O T A D L Z S C A R F T
L N R B R O N P I I N R R S
S S T O O R C A A P L D O E
I T C W H Y E N B J P K C V
K H O T E S E T I L A E K E
A G L I Q E W S A A A M R E
H I L E Z Z D U R E R Z A L
K T A I L O R I K E W B E S
R Y R S K I R T S S J S J R
```

Auto Racing

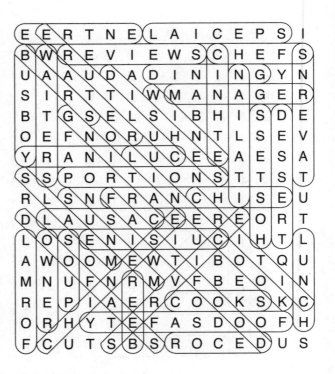

Tiles

Elvis

Restaurants

362

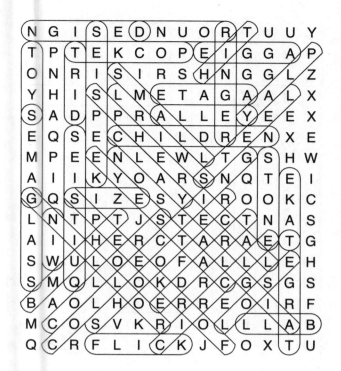

Marbles

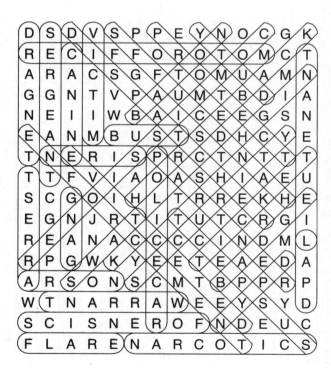

Wine Tour

The Scientific Method

Police

Parenthood

Sea Life

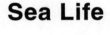

Spicy

Canning

Trees

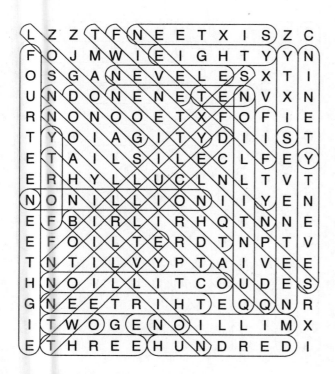

Numerical

State Fair

Car Parts

The Game of Kings

Best Actress

Roofs

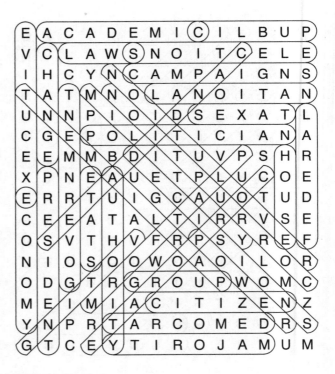

Political

Telling Time

Pixar

Hospital

Skiing

160

SUPERSIZED PUZZLES!

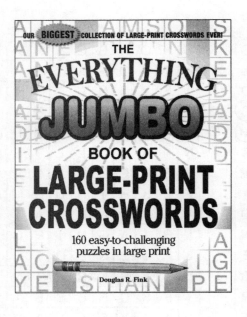
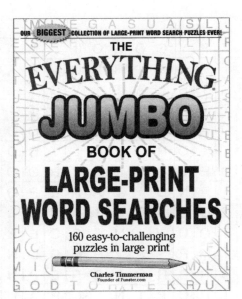